The Con Men

PEARSON

At Pearson, we take learning personally. Our courses and resources are available as books, online and via multi-lingual packages, helping people learn whatever, wherever and however they choose.

We work with leading authors to develop the strongest learning experiences, bringing cutting-edge thinking and best learning practice to a global market. We craft our print and digital resources to do more to help learners not only understand their content, but to see it in action and apply what they learn, whether studying or at work.

Pearson is the world's leading learning company. Our portfolio includes Penguin, Dorling Kindersley, the Financial Times and our educational business, Pearson International. We are also a leading provider of electronic learning programmes and of test development, processing and scoring services to educational institutions, corporations and professional bodies around the world.

Every day our work helps learning flourish, and wherever learning flourishes, so do people.

To learn more please visit us at: **www.pearson.com/uk**

The Con Men

Leo Gough

A history of financial fraud and the
lessons you can learn

PEARSON

Harlow, England • London • New York • Boston • San Francisco • Toronto • Sydney
Auckland • Singapore • Hong Kong • Tokyo • Seoul • Taipei • New Delhi
Cape Town • São Paulo • Mexico City • Madrid • Amsterdam • Munich • Paris • Milan

Pearson Education Limited
Edinburgh Gate
Harlow CM20 2JE
United Kingdom
Tel: +44 (0)1279 623623
Web: www.pearson.com/uk

First published 2013 (print and electronic)

ISBN: 978-0-273-75134-2 (print)
       978-0-273-75177-9 (PDF)
       978-0-273-75178-6 (ePub)

British Library Cataloguing-in-Publication Data
A catalog record for the print edition is available from the British Library

Library of Congress Cataloging-in-Publication Data
Gough, Leo.
  The con men / Leo Gough.
     pages cm
  Includes index.
  ISBN 978-0-273-75134-2 (pbk.) -- ISBN 978-0-273-75177-9 (PDF) -- ISBN 978-0-273-75178-6 (ePub)
  1. Commercial crimes--History. 2. Fraud--History. 3. Financial institutions--Corrupt practices--History.
  4. Commercial crimes--United States--History. 5. Fraud--United States--History. 6. Financial
  institutions--Corrupt practices--United States--History. I. Title.
  HV6768.G689 2013
  364.16'30973--dc23
                          2013020115

The Financial Times. With a worldwide network of highly respected journalists, *The Financial Times* provides global business news, insightful opinion and expert analysis of business, finance and politics. With over 500 journalists reporting from 50 countries worldwide, our in-depth coverage of international news is objectively reported and analysed from an independent, global perspective. To find out more, visit www.ft.com/pearsonoffer.

10 9 8 7 6 5 4 3 2 1
17 16 15 14 13

Cover design by Kit Foster
Print edition typeset in 10pt Gilliard Std by 30
Print edition printed and bound in Great Britain by Ashford Colour Press Ltd, Gosport, Hants

NOTE THAT ANY PAGE CROSS-REFERENCES REFER TO THE PRINT EDITION

For A.B.

Contents

About the author

Leo Gough is the author of more than 20 books on personal finance and investment, some of which have appeared in translation in German, Japanese, Chinese, Russian, Italian and Portuguese. Some of these include: *How The Stock Market Really Works*, *The Financial Times Guide to Business Numeracy*, *Going Offshore*, *25 Investment Classics*; *The Finance Manual for Non-Financial Managers*; *Financial Times Guide to Selecting Shares that Perform* (co-authored most recent edition with Richard Koch). Since 1997 he has spent much of his time in the Asia/Pacific region, working with banks, consultancy firms and publishers to produce investment books and research for this dynamically expanding region.

Acknowledgements

Research for this book has relied principally upon court cases that have resulted in convictions, and upon public enquiries into financial scandals. The increasing willingness of governments, financial regulators and the courts on both sides of the Atlantic to make these materials publicly accessible via the internet has greatly increased the transparency of these murky affairs. In particular, C-SPAN (the Cable-Satellite Public Affairs Network in the US) and the UK's Parliament TV now provide thousands of hours of archived witness testimony and cross-examination via the internet that enable anyone to study these complex issues at first hand – I applaud the democratic impulse behind this development, which is a genuine boon to the private investor. Christopher Cudmore, Editor in Chief of Professional Publishing at Pearson Education, was untiring in his encouragement, and retained his faith in the book even when it seemed that it would never be finished; I am extremely grateful to him for his tolerance, advice and unwavering support.

Introduction

Investors have very short memories.
Roman Abramovich, Russian billionaire

n the days before electronic point-of-sale tills, when you spent an evening in a bar with some friends you could try the following experiment: check the total cost of the drinks each time your group bought a round to see if the prices were consistent. Very often they were not, even though the drinks bought didn't vary. Why did this happen and who was to blame? Perhaps it was because the bar staff weren't very good at maths, and we should blame the State for allowing so many individuals to leave school without adequate numeracy skills. Perhaps the place was understaffed, and the bartenders were hopelessly overworked, leading to errors – in which case, presumably, we should blame the management and, if we are so inclined, the evil effects of alcohol on the customers who tended to become more and more demanding as the evening progressed. Let's go out on a limb here: perhaps it was because some of the bar staff were overcharging for some rounds of drinks and pocketing the difference. Old-fashioned people would call that theft.

There are some similarities here with the financial services industry, which has come under attack in recent years, particularly since the banking crisis of 2008, for a whole range of shortcomings. Around the world it has expanded hugely since the 1980s, leading to a kind of consumerised capitalism in which armies of poorly trained staff have often missold and misdescribed investment products. Deregulation forced sleepy institutions to become aggressively competitive just to survive in the new environment. Also, customers, who were always quite greedy, seem to be becoming more so; for example, in some senses we, the public, 'deserved' the 2008 banking crisis because we took advantage of all the easy credit and we didn't throw out the politicians who should and could have prevented the crisis.

This book isn't really about those shortcomings, although they often come into the story. It's about outright financial fraud, committed by individuals on a grand scale. This is where the bar analogy starts to break down. A barman is stealing from both you and his employers when he overcharges you, but he can only pocket the difference between what he charges you and the real price. In financial services it is sometimes possible to take much, much more, and it's not only the workers at the bottom of the food chain who sometimes steal. In financial services, the people who can steal the most are often the bosses of the business.

For example, in 2009 Bernard Madoff, a former chairman of the NASDAQ stock exchange, well-known for his philanthropy and much admired for the success of his long-established stock brokerage firm, was convicted of defrauding his clients of almost $65 billion. In the same year, Sir Robert Allen Stanford, a Texan, was stripped of his Antiguan knighthood as US regulators began proceedings against him alleging his involvement in an $8 billion fraud of clients of his Stanford International Bank. In 2006, Kenneth Lay, CEO of Enron, the giant US energy company, was convicted on 19 counts of fraud, including false accounting and insider trading. Investors in Enron's corporate bonds were outraged that the firm continued to be rated as AAA until only four days before its bankruptcy. In 2003, Parmalat, the Italian food conglomerate, collapsed owing $20 billion; its founder, the millionaire art-lover Calisto Tanzi, is currently serving a prison sentence for embezzlement and false accounting. In 2002, Worldcom, a US telecoms company, filed for bankruptcy, losing investors an estimated $100 billion; its former CEO, Bernie Ebbers, is serving 25 years for securities fraud and false accounting. In short, large-scale frauds occur frequently – they are not as rare as shocked media reports about the latest scandal can make them seem.

Investors who are victimised in large frauds rarely get all their money back; in fact, they often don't get any of their money back. This book is primarily intended for investors who are interested in avoiding being abused in this way, but it will also be of interest to people who don't invest in the stock market at all, because, as we will see, fraud and other financial misdeeds are sometimes so severe that they end up affecting the whole economy, not only of a particular country but also the whole world. For example, at the time of writing it is very hard in the UK to get a mortgage, even though a few years ago it was very easy; fraudulent practices in the sub-prime lending boom in the US in 2007 was a major factor in the series of events that led to this situation, where ordinary people in the UK are suffering. And we can spare a thought for the people of Greece, whose economy is currently in dire straits, in part because of long-term fraudulent accounting by their own government.

Sadly, governments don't usually go to jail for fraud; the worst that can happen in a Western democracy is that the politicians get voted out. And as the excellent documentary film *Inside Job,* winner of the 2010 Academy Award for best documentary, has demonstrated, dishonest practices in financial services can be systemic, running like a fungus through government, government agencies, regulatory bodies, boards of directors, banks, corporations and even into academia. One of the most interesting aspects of the film was that it showed for the first time just how some senior academic economists (who in America can flit between university, boardrooms and government) had helped to provide a phoney intellectual justification for the financial excesses that were occurring, and they were in the pockets of the banks and corporations, which were profiting the most from the excesses. These academics knew better; they should have called for it to stop. Instead, they backed up a reckless free-for-all that they knew had to end in disaster. And before you assume that *Inside Job* was made by a bunch of fuzzy-minded political extremists, you should know that the director, Charles Ferguson, has a PhD in political science from MIT, started a software company he sold to Microsoft for $130 million, and says of himself,

'I don't think I'm an anti-capitalist or anti-business at all. I am, however, against large-scale criminality and if being against gigantic frauds makes me left wing, then so be it.' Ferguson is hardly a bomb-throwing anarchist!

This book can offer no solutions to these grander socio-political problems. What it can do, however, is to show how big-time fraudsters – the ones who actually do go to jail – take advantage of opportunities to commit fraud on a large scale, and to suggest ways in which you might be able to spot a fraud and avoid it before it's too late. The twelve chapters of the book are organised into four parts. The first part introduces some of the major frauds that have occurred during the last few decades to provide insight into the ways in which specific types of fraud tend to run in fashions, depending on the economic and political circumstances. The second part deals in more detail with the mechanics of particular frauds, and the third part takes a closer look at the ways in which investors, and the financial industry itself, can become vulnerable to fraud. In the final part, the focus is on the ways in which we, ordinary private investors, can protect ourselves against being victimised by fraudsters.

So, in Chapter 1, let's look first at two of the most recent villains whose activities should and could have been stopped before they got so wildly out of hand: Bernie Madoff and Allen Stanford.

PART ONE

A brief but efficient history of trickery

1

The horror stories

Bernie Madoff

In today's regulatory environment, it's virtually impossible to violate the rules.

Bernard Madoff

Bernie Madoff was sentenced to 150 years' imprisonment in 2009 for running a massive Ponzi scheme. We'll discuss the anatomy of Ponzi schemes in more detail in Chapter 3; in essence they are fraudulent schemes in which the fraudster pays investors their returns out of the money he is obtaining from new investors, rather than from genuine investment returns. Here's the basic story of the Madoff affair: at the height of the US economic crisis in 2008 Bernie Madoff, a former chairman of NASDAQ (a major US stock market), was denounced to the authorities by his two sons for swindling a large number of investors, many of them wealthy, by running a fraudulent investment management business in which he produced false account statements for clients showing fictitious investment returns and funded any withdrawals out of other clients' money. Many investors were unaware that their money was with Madoff because they had invested in funds operated by other firms that 'fed' Madoff's fund with money (and are thus called 'feeder funds'), often without informing their clients of this fact.

The vast scale of the fraud, the incompetence of the regulators, and behaviour of other market players with regard to Madoff, provide many insights into the dangers facing private investors, and we will examine various aspects of the case throughout this book.

> The vast scale of the fraud, the incompetence of the regulators, and behaviour of other market players with regard to Madoff, provide many insights into the dangers facing private investors

Madoff had started his first business in Wall Street in 1960, and by the time of his sentencing he owned three apparently solid financial services operations: a stock broker, a proprietary trading firm (for trading on the firm's own account), and an investment adviser. What few people knew, until the collapse, was that for at least two decades Madoff had been running a gigantic Ponzi scheme through his investment advice firm. In December 2008 Madoff, then 69, had a meeting with his two middle-aged sons, Mark and Andrew, at which he confessed that he had been falsifying his clients' investment returns for years, that the family was ruined and he expected to go to jail. He asked his sons to wait a few days before reporting him to the authorities so that he could disburse funds to various relatives and associates. Justice was relatively swift, and in March of 2009 Madoff made what appeared to be a full confession before a judge and received his sentence without standing trial.

The staggering scale of the fraud meant that the issue didn't go away and, during the following years more and more information came to light. Initially, great attention was paid to the failure of regulators, especially the SEC (Securities and Exchange Commission), to act against Madoff in spite of the fact that they had received a number of credible complaints, dating back to 1992, there was something seriously wrong with Madoff's operation. The most active of the complainers, the investment analyst Harry Markopoulos, emerged from obscurity to produce striking evidence that despite repeated efforts over several years, his denunciations of Madoff's activities had been virtually ignored by the SEC (for a full discussion, see Chapter 3). Although it has now been satisfactorily established that Madoff's scam dated back at least as far as the early 1990s, as he claimed in his confession, there are strong suspicions it may have begun much earlier in the 1960s when Madoff was just starting out.

Allen Stanford

I would die and go to hell if it is a Ponzi scheme. It's no Ponzi scheme.
R. Allen Stanford, CEO Stanford Financial Group
(currently serving 150 years for running a Ponzi scheme)

In 2002 star investment salesman Charles Hazlett left his job at Prudential Securities to join the Miami office of Stanford Group Company, a financial services firm that was a part of the Stanford Financial Group, a network of privately held companies controlled by the billionaire Texan entrepreneur R. Allen Stanford. Like Stanford, his ultimate boss, Hazlett is a tall man, confidence-inspiring and with a thunderously loud voice.

The job offer had been too good to pass up: an annual salary of $180,000, a fabulous office overlooking the Miami waterfront, and a promise of up to $400,000 in bonuses. Hazlett got stuck in, selling what Stanford had to offer to investors, and within a matter of months he had become one of the firm's top salespeople, earning a $100,000 BMW as a bonus. In the course of his discussions with his customers a number of questions had come up for which Hazlett was unable to obtain satisfactory answers from the firm. Why, for example, was the firm able to offer investors Certificates of Deposit (CDs) with rates of return higher than were available elsewhere? Why was the firm pushing this form of investment so hard? Why was the auditing being done by a tiny outfit? Why were the sales commissions on the sale of these CDs so much higher than the average commission rate for similar products? And, crucially, where was the firm investing the deposits it received from its customers?

Hazlett managed to get a meeting with Stanford's young Chief Investment Officer, Laura Pendergest, then 28, but was unable to obtain any concrete answers from her; the meeting ended with Pendergest fleeing from the room in tears. Shortly afterwards, according to Hazlett, the Chief Financial Officer, James D. Davis, telephoned him and 'was not very nice to me'. Hazlett soon left the firm; he had sold $17 million dollars' worth of CDs during his time there, but called all of his clients to warn them to remove their money from Stanford.

The 2005 annual report of the main banking arm of the group, Stanford International Group Ltd, has a celebratory, though reassuring, tone. '20 years, $4 billion in total assets, and we still serve our first client', runs a slogan on page 2. An anodyne statement from the bank's Chairman, Allen Stanford, marvels at the pace of financial change around the world during the bank's 20-year life and attributes the bank's success in growing 'from a few hundred clients in a handful of countries' in 1985 into 'a multibillion dollar institution that today serves over 35,000 clients in 102 countries around the globe' to, among other things, 'our ability to attract the best talent in the financial services industry' and 'our consistent profitability'.

To the average reader, there is nothing immediately suspect about the report. It is no more gushing than many other banks' reports, and its emphasis on its human face and its dedication to honesty and personal service must have been appealing at a time when many banks seemed to be becoming increasingly depersonalised. But what of the bank's location offshore, on a Caribbean island? Vice-president Eugene Kipper, pictured on page 12 of the report, had an explanation: 'the Bank is domiciled in a well-regulated, low-tax jurisdiction'. It may be a matter of taste, but for the average investor in the US or Europe, no offshore tax haven is likely to offer quite the same level of investor protection as is provided in their own countries. And as events were to show, Antigua's regulators were not all that they should have been (as we will see in Chapter 5).

In February 2009, the SEC, which had been investigating Stanford's operations almost continuously since the 1980s, finally acted, filing a suit against Stanford in Texas for conducting 'a massive Ponzi scheme' and obtaining a court injunction to freeze the Stanford Financial Group's assets. In April 2009 ABC news caught up with Stanford outside a Houston restaurant, where he declared tearfully, 'I would die and go to hell if it's a Ponzi scheme. It's no Ponzi scheme', and he continued to declare his innocence throughout his trial, saying, when he was sentenced to 110 years in prison on 14 June 2012, that he was not a thief and had not intended to defraud anyone. At the time of writing the Stanford story continues to play out. As already mentioned, Allen Stanford was sentenced to 110 years (in 2010 he received a savage beating in prison – apparently because he was hogging the phone) but a host of other lawsuits have not yet been resolved, including the trials of other key associates in Stanford's operations.

Could you have spotted a problem?

Madoff and Stanford were two very different characters, but in their own individual ways they seemed, superficially at least, likeable and plausible. They inspired confidence, at least in the people who chose to invest with them – and that, of course, is an essential quality in a confidence trickster. The trouble is, all investment businesses that take money from the public must inspire confidence. How can you tell the difference between someone like Warren Buffett, the doyen of investors, who, the present writer believes, is a truly honest man, and someone like Bernie Madoff, who merely *seemed* to be an honest man? It's really rather difficult, especially if you don't have the numerical and analytical skills to penetrate the financial information about a firm.

Bernie Madoff's hypocrisy beggared belief. For example, in a public panel discussion in 2007, he said:

> ... *by and large in today's regulatory environment, it's virtually impossible to violate the rules. This is something that the public really doesn't understand. If you read things in the newspaper and you see somebody violate a rule, you say well, they're always doing this. But it's impossible for a violation to go undetected, certainly not for a considerable period of time.*

Paternal, relaxed, knowledgeable, modest, reassuring – that was how Bernie seemed, and is what many investors want. If you had been present at the discussion, could you really have guessed that Madoff had been running a Ponzi scheme the whole time?

In his own way, Allen Stanford was equally reassuring. He claimed that he lived frugally, but in addition to the vast sums he lavished on his corporate offices and developments in Antigua, which included building a huge complex next to the airport through which Stanford clients could pass without customs checks, he spent a lot on his own lifestyle. Between 2000 and 2002 he spent more than $400,000 on clothes at a Beverly Hills store, built a series of mansions in various countries, and purchased a string of private jets and boats, including a British naval frigate. Stanford knew how to live large, and he knew how to make the people around him feel good. As the business expanded, he became increasingly more ambitious in his public relations, giving frequent interviews to *Forbes* magazine and TV stations, and making a commencement address at the University of Houston.

For the British, Allen Stanford only swam into public view with his entry into the world of cricket. Like many non-US sports, cricket has gone without the dubious benefits of massive commercialisation bestowed on baseball and American football. In 2008, having built a fabulous cricket ground in Antigua (hugely popular with the locals), complete with a restaurant/sports bar called 'The Sticky Wicket', Stanford set up a $20 million winner-takes-all cricket match between England and a West Indian team. The match was part of the Twenty20 scheme, in which each side only has one innings, and the entire match lasts only between 3 and 4 hours. Stanford's team won. He then struck a deal with the English Cricket Board (ECB) to pump some £11.4 million into the English game over five years. Eyebrows were raised, however, at the sight of Stanford carousing at a match in Antigua in the company of the English cricketers' 'WAGs', one of whom was televised sitting on Stanford's knee.

In general, Antiguans seem to have welcomed Allen Stanford's financial domination of the island, mainly because he spent so lavishly on community projects and had become the largest private employer. He took Antiguan nationality in 2006 while retaining his US nationality and received a knighthood (Antigua and Barbuda is an independent constitutional monarchy whose head of state is Queen Elizabeth; its government thus has the right to recommend candidates for such honours). Locals ignored obvious questions about his modus operandi and the origin of his vast wealth, assuming, perhaps, that the US would probably get him in the end, but in the meantime he was doing more good than harm on the island.

Lessons from the past

Although the Madoff and Stanford scandals occurred at a time when overly lax regulations had allowed the financial services industry to drag the world into a serious financial crisis, neither of the two men are really typical of what was going wrong in the industry at the time. Neither Madoff nor Stanford were really 'insiders' with regard to the dubious practices that had become systemic in the investment banking world during the 'noughties'. While they benefited from a period during which the main financial regulators, in particular the Securities and Exchange Commission (SEC), the main US market regulator, were unusually incompetent (see Chapters 3 and 5), their fraudulent operations had little in common with the misdeeds of the wider industry. Although the frauds were discovered during the financial crisis, they were not discovered because of investigations in response to the crisis, but because the market crash made it increasingly difficult for the fraudsters to conceal the shaky foundations of their schemes.

In previous crises, by contrast, the major fraudsters have often been seen as typifying the mode of wrongdoing of the time. During the 1990s, for example, the development of the internet gave rise to the 'dotcom' boom, during which a large number of internet-related companies became grossly overvalued as canny venture capitalists launched the firms on the stock market in Initial Public Offerings (IPOs) into which enthusiastic investors poured their money, even though many of these firms were not making any profits. There were, of course, some notable survivors, such as Amazon, but many of these firms had collapsed by the year 2000. Two iconic scandals, Enron (discussed in detail in Chapter 11), and Worldcom, came to be seen as symbolic of the dotcom bust; both firms had committed massive accounting fraud in an effort to prevent their share prices from dropping. Although neither firm was truly an internet start-up (Enron had started out as a Texan oil and gas company while Worldcom had grown to become the second largest telecoms company in America through a series of mergers and acquisitions during the 1990s), they were associated with the dotcom bubble because they were two really large firms, with apparently sizeable revenues, that appeared to demonstrate money could be made now, not just in the future, by internet-based businesses.

Investment booms generally begin for sound reasons: for instance, a technological innovation, perhaps coupled with a change in the regulatory regime, may emerge that people are clearly going to want, and early investors attempt to pick the operations which seem the most likely to scoop up a large chunk of the new business being created. In the 1840s, for example, the introduction of a railway system to Britain was clearly going to transform ordinary people's lives, radically reduce transportation time and costs, make new conurbations and industrial arrangements possible, and so on. This was no illusion, but, during the Railway Mania of the 1840s, investors rushed to put their money into the new railway companies that were being formed, creating a feverish, over-optimistic atmosphere in which higher and higher prices were being paid for projects of poorer and poorer quality. Some of these railway projects were outright frauds from the beginning, others committed fraud when things began to go wrong, and still others completed their projects but found them to be less lucrative than they had hoped.

So it was for the dotcom boom of the 1990s. The underlying premise, that the expansion of the internet was going to create enormous efficiencies for both industry and the public, was perfectly sound, as were some of the businesses created to take advantage of the new opportunities. The trouble was, as both deserving and undeserving dotcom start-ups began to change hands for ridiculously high prices, it became increasingly difficult for investors to sort the wheat from the chaff, in an atmosphere of jargon-ridden, staggeringly arrogant 'new economy' talk emanating from venture capitalists, stock analysts, internet CEOs and other interested parties.

Worldcom began life in 1983 as Long Distance Discount Services (LDDS), which was set up by a group of private investors, including Bernie Ebbers, the future CEO, to take advantage of the deregulation of the telecommunications industry, which involved the selling off of many telecoms assets. LDDS made a living by buying long-distance telecoms capacity at wholesale prices from the main carriers such as AT&T and selling a long-distance call service at retail. Bernie Ebbers drove LDDS to grow by the aggressive purchase of other long-distance providers during the 1990s, changing the firm's name to Worldcom in 1995.

Hailed as a 'revolutionary' and a 'visionary', Ebbers aimed to create a new kind of telecoms giant that would be able to offer the whole range of voice and data network services in a single, seamless digital package. In 1997, Ebbers moved in on a deal in which British Telecom was attempting to purchase MCI Communications for $19 billion; Ebbers offered $30 billion. When the deal went through, Worldcom had become one of the dominant telecoms players in the US. Wall Street loved it; Worldcom's spending spree was driven by its ever-increasing stock price, and it looked as though Ebbers had got the formula right, as the firm bought up major internet providers, such as UUNET, fibre optic cable networks and other new capacity in preparation for the eagerly awaited communications revolution.

Between 1994 and the third quarter of 1999 (just before the MCI merger) the firm had enjoyed virtually uninterrupted growth in sales, and its share price had risen from $8.17 in early 1994 to $47.91 (adjusted for stock splits). Much depended on meeting Wall Street expectations in its quarterly figures, as this would help keep the share price up and facilitate further acquisitions. Worldcom fell foul of anti-trust (anti-monopoly) laws when pursuing its next target, Sprint, and the deal fell through in 2000. The failure of the Sprint acquisition signalled that mega-mergers were no longer going to be possible, and the firm would have to seek growth in other ways. The telecoms business was becoming less profitable, however, as competition increased and a glut in communications capacity began to develop. Worldcom's share price had dropped to $18.94 by 1 November 2000. In 2001 the whole sector's sales income and share prices dropped as it became clear that the glut in capacity would remain for years. In spite of the problems in the industry, Worldcom's figures continued to meet Wall Street expectations of high sales growth. Finally, early in 2002, Worldcom had to release its fourth quarter 2001 results, which for the first time failed to meet analysts' expectations. Ebbers put out optimistic messages, but had to resign in April. In June the firm announced that there were important irregularities in its accounts, and its shares were suspended.

What had been going on? According to prosecutors, as the telecoms sector began to go bad in 1999, Bernie Ebbers and a handful of senior executives came under great pressure to keep all the company news sounding good. Worldcom's main expense was its 'line costs', meaning the price it had to pay for carrying a call from its starting point to its end point. Starting in 1999, Worldcom bosses started to reduce the reported line costs, keeping them to a ratio of 42% of gross income (which is what the Wall Street analysts were expecting). The real line costs were rising to above 50% of gross income, but the Worldcom insiders kept the reported costs down by using a number of improper methods; between 1999 and 2002, the firm hid more than $7 billion in line costs illegally. More than $3 billion of this was done by improperly 'releasing' sums of money, known as accruals, that had been set aside against expected future bills from suppliers. At the end of 2000, running out of these accruals, Worldcom bosses began to mark line costs as capital investments, rather than what they really were, suppliers' services that had to be paid for; this manoeuvre was quite outside normal accounting practice, and had the added effect of making Worldcom appear to be profitable, when it was in fact beginning to suffer losses.

Bernie Ebbers, along with Worldcom's CFO, Scott Sullivan, told Wall Street analysts that Worldcom was able to sustain its high growth rates because it could manage the industry-wide problems, by implication, better than its competitors could. Worldcom's external auditors, the large firm Arthur Andersen, did not pick up any of the accounting problems; they were uncovered by three mid-level internal accountants, employees of Worldcom, who, between April and June 2002, conducted a clandestine investigation that revealed some $3.8 billion in misallocated items.

From the private investor's point of view, the real scandal in the Worldcom affair was that allegedly independent experts, on whose opinions we have to rely, seem to have been asleep at the wheel. We rely on independent auditors to check that the accounts are accurate, and in this case Worldcom's auditors, Arthur Andersen, failed to discover the problems. We rely on stock market analysts to apply their expertise appropriately and provide an honest assessment of the outlook for the company as an investment. In the late 1990s, Jack Grubman, senior telecoms analyst at the investment bank Smith Barney and widely regarded as an industry guru, continuously endorsed Worldcom even as its situation was worsening. Grubman was later banned for life from the securities industry by the SEC for producing misleading reports on a number of firms in the telecoms sector.

If you can't trust the analysts and the auditors, who can you trust?

The answer is, of course, that it is all a matter of degree. You can trust some governments more than others, for example. The UK government can probably be trusted not to help itself to the contents of your savings accounts, but the Italian government did just this some years ago during a crisis. You can probably trust the major UK high street banks not to break the main banking regulations affecting consumers; the same could not be said for banks like Landsbanki (the Icelandic bank behind the Icesave scheme that collapsed in 2008) or BCCI (a large international bank that collapsed in 1991 leaving thousands of UK savers high and dry).

> You can probably rely on your own accountant to tell the truth about your own accounts, but major accountancy firms, such as Arthur Andersen, have on occasion completely failed to spot accounting fraud in large companies they were auditing.

You can probably rely on your own accountant to tell the truth about your own accounts, but major accountancy firms, such as Arthur Andersen, have on occasion completely failed to spot accounting fraud in large companies they were auditing. At every level of the investment industry, and in the firms listed on the stock market, we can find examples of wrongdoing. These examples are not isolated, random occurrences; the type of fraud varies according to the opportunities available during a particular period, and frauds tend to be discovered in the aftermath of a market collapse, but at all times there is a danger of some kind of fraud. 'Let the buyer beware' is good, if not very reassuring, advice, and investors need to take some responsibility for the decisions they take. Protection is better for mass-market investment products, but returns may be lower and charges higher. Not every investment deal offers good value in terms of the trade-off between safety and risk (in fact, fraudsters often exploit the public's confusion about this). Investors who would rather hand over their money to a reassuring, avuncular figure may find that they have trusted, say, a Bernie Madoff. As investors we need to develop our own skills, and our own antennae, to improve our ability to detect possible frauds. As the buyers, we have one great advantage: we can say 'No' and walk away. Any time that you feel you must invest quickly before the opportunity vanishes, the chances are you are not making a good investment; it is exactly this fear of missing out on something wonderful which drives investment booms, and forces share prices of fashionable companies and industries through the roof.

2

Our touching need for confidence

People think you have to be brilliant to be an investment banker,
but it's not rocket science.

Dennis Levine, investment banker jailed in 1987 for insider dealing

If investors believed that the entire financial services industry was crooked and that an outsider would always be cheated, what would happen? All other factors remaining equal, investors would simply stop putting their money into financial investments. Money would flow out of shares, bonds, derivatives and cash deposits and into some other type of asset such as residential property. But that has not happened in the major financial markets. On the contrary, they have massively expanded during the last 40 years, and millions of new investors from all over the world have entered the financial markets, directly or indirectly. This process could not have occurred if all investors were continuously defrauded. And, of course, they are not – by and large, investors are dealt with relatively honestly by the financial services industry, although they are often overcharged for the products and services they buy.

In this chapter we will go back a few decades to look at two major investment scandals, the Dennis Levine/Ivan Boesky insider trading scandal of the 1980s and the larger-than-life Caribbean scheming of Robert Vesco in the

1970s. Although times have changed and the particular scams that these men operated would not, at present, be likely to succeed, they shed light on the capacity and limitations of the regulatory system, especially when it has to contend with people who set out to defeat it by operating, in part, abroad.

Investors are particularly sensitive to problems with certain types of investment product, and governments and, accordingly, investment firms are particularly careful to regulate them in a way that is both perceived to be fair and provides investors with a return. Thus, a savings account at a high street bank in the UK, for example, is well protected by compensation schemes and government regulation and, even more importantly, by the will of successive governments to make sure that investors get most, if not all, of their money back in the event of a collapse. UK investors in Icesave, the Icelandic online savings account that went broke in 2008, might not have received compensation from the Icelandic government, so the UK government stepped in quickly to compensate them, taking on the burden of a protracted row with Iceland over liability. This robust protection is a public good; we all benefit from being able to live in a country where you can be confident that your bank savings are not suddenly going to go up in smoke.

Most people would not expect to enjoy the same level of protection if they invested in less standardised investments. If you buy shares in a high-tech firm when it first comes to market, for instance, you know that you are taking on a wider set of risks than if you put the money in a savings account – and, especially, the investment might lose money or even turn out to be worthless. And if you are a very experienced investor – perhaps a market professional – you are expected to have the psychological equivalent of cauliflower ears and a broken nose and be able to tolerate losses in much more unpredictable and volatile investments, such as derivatives or shares in obscure, illiquid stock markets. There is, in other words, a kind of hierarchy of protection, with the strongest protection for ordinary members of the public who are encouraged to invest in safe investments producing a modest return, and the lightest protection for big-time players who are very active in the international markets.

At every level, from the humble gilt holder to the big-time financial plunger, the market needs to have confidence that, broadly speaking and most of the time, transactions are performed honestly, payments arrive on time, and financial information is accurate. A very important factor in maintaining market confidence is a high volume of transactions, which provides liquidity. On the other hand, 'thinly traded' markets, which means markets where there are only a few, infrequent transactions, do not inspire confidence, principally because prices tend to jump wildly from one transaction to the next; there is also the suspicion, justified in many cases, in thin markets that there are insiders who are trying to manipulate the game.

Insider trading

The major stock markets function by trying to ensure that all listed companies announce key information publicly, so that everyone in the market hears about it at the same time. Insider trading means trading on information that is non-public – if you are the employee of a listed firm or an investment bank, say, and you learn during your work that Company X has had a disastrous quarter it will announce tomorrow, it is insider trading, illegal in many markets – to rush out and sell your Company X shares before the announcement. It is also illegal for you to tell a friend who then makes the transaction. Why is this illegal? It might look, after all, like a victimless crime – you make a profit on the deal, and no one is the wiser. The reason is that insider dealing is a kind of stealing; the victims are the other investors involved who have not been able to benefit from the inside information and, by taking a profit on a deal you are, in effect, taking something from them, just as you would if you took money from, say, an office Christmas-party fund or any other sum of money that was being held on behalf of a group of people.

There is some theoretical controversy about insider trading. Some academics, for example the monetarist economist Milton Friedman, have argued that insider trading benefits the market as a whole by increasing its efficiency: if the directors of Company X suddenly start buying as many shares as they can in their company, this insider buying will soon be noticed (directors have to disclose such transactions) by the market, which will respond accordingly. Thus, the argument goes, insider dealing is just one of the many competitive forces that ensures price-sensitive information will reach the market as quickly as possible. There may be something in this argument, but investors do not like to feel that some insider, with special information, has been able to profit at their expense, and in many countries at least some forms of insider dealing are now illegal.

Ivan Boesky and Dennis Levine

During the 1970s stock market regulation was quite heavily enforced, but in the 1980s the emphasis changed, especially in the US, where the SEC (the Securities and Exchange Commission, the main US stock market regulator) aggressively pursued investigations and prosecutions of financial wrongdoers. In the 1980s there was a boom in company mergers and acquisitions, providing enormous opportunities for individuals to make quick profits by insider dealing, which developed rapidly into an epidemic.

Drexel Burnham Lambert was an investment bank at the heart of the merger mania, and one of its employees, Dennis Levine, was one of the largest insider dealers ever uncovered. Levine had met Robert Wilkis, then a lending officer at Citibank, in the 1970s, and when they later found themselves both working in Europe, they became intrigued by the lack of prohibitions against insider trading in many European countries. The pair both had access to price-sensitive information through their jobs, and decided to open bank accounts in Switzerland to trade on this information secretly. They agreed to share information with each other, but that they would trade separately to avoid discovery. When he wanted to buy or sell securities, Levine would telephone his Swiss bank from a public telephone, using a codename, and give his order. Many of the trades were staggeringly simple; one or other of the duo would hear some information about a company that would positively affect the share price when it became public – for example, that another firm was launching a takeover bid against it – and then Wilkis and Levine would purchase shares in the target firm, selling later after the takeover bid had been announced and the shares in the target company had consequently gone up. According to Levine, even though he researched the information carefully after receiving it, some of his investments suffered losses. Overall, however, Levine made money, building $39,750 up to $11.5 million through insider trading once or twice a month over a seven-year period. After some time Levine's Swiss bankers asked him to move his account, and he switched to another Swiss bank, Bank Leu, at its subsidiary in the Bahamas.

An important innovation of the 1980s was the introduction of a liquid market in 'junk bonds' by Michael Milken, a financier at Drexel Burnham Lambert. Junk bonds are simply company bonds that for one reason or another have been deemed to be below investment grade. Junk bonds tend to produce a higher yield (the equivalent of interest) because they are considered to be higher risk, and Milken's initial innovation was to show that many junk bonds belonging to 'fallen angels' (companies whose financial situation had worsened since their issue of investment grade bonds) were in fact worth considerably more than their current valuation. Later, as the junk bond market grew, Milken and Drexel began to use them as a financing mechanism in mergers and acquisitions, arranging for the issue of bonds that were graded as 'junk' at the outset and finding willing buyers for them. Each year, a 'Predators' Ball' was held in Beverly Hills that attracted the movers and shakers in the mergers and acquisitions (M&A) business, including the predators themselves (corporate raiders like Ron Perelman and Carl Icahn), institutional buyers of junk bonds, and senior managers from companies interested in M&A. One of the star guests was Ivan Boesky, known as an 'arbitrageur' who specialised in making speculative profits in merger plays; Levine met Boesky at the Predators' Ball of 1985, and soon they were exchanging information about the market.

According to Levine, at first there was no acknowledgement that any of the information might be 'insider', but eventually Boesky offered to give Levine a percentage of the profits he was making. According to Levine, 'Despite my own illicit activities, I was flabbergasted. I couldn't believe he would risk exposing himself so blatantly, by proposing something clearly illegal on its face.' Levine claims not to know why he eventually agreed to cooperate with Boesky for money. The SEC alleged that the deal was to give Levine 5% of profits Boesky made using Levine's information, and 1% of the profits he made if he maintained or increased an existing holding. Levine provided insider information on various deals, including the merger of Nabisco and RJ Reynolds, and a bid for Houston Natural Gas by InterNorth. Unknown to Levine, Boesky was also paying others for insider information, including Martin Siegel, a senior executive at Drexel, who was a major architect of mergers during the 1980s, and had been secretly receiving suitcases full of cash from Boesky in return for juicy tips. Boesky, known for his 'uncanny' ability to spot which companies would be the target of a takeover bid, became the subject of the SEC's interest when it became clear that he was making huge profits on nearly every major merger he speculated in (for instance, he netted $28 million on Nestlé's take-over of Carnation). For the SEC, Boesky's success as a speculator was just too good to be true, but they could not find any evidence of wrongdoing.

Then, in July 1985, Merrill Lynch passed on to the SEC an anonymous letter claiming that two of the firm's brokers in Venezuela were committing insider trading offences. According to Levine, bankers at Bank Leu in the Bahamas had been copying Levine's trades – apparently because they guessed that Levine was trading on inside information – and had been using Merrill Lynch for their own transactions. Brokers at Merrill Lynch appeared to have been copying the Bank Leu trades and had attracted suspicion. The SEC conducted a ten-month investigation, but Bank Leu refused to divulge any information about the suspect accounts. The SEC applied legal pressure on the bank until it finally agreed, in May 1986, to give the SEC the name of the account holder in question: it was Dennis Levine.

SEC pressure on Dennis Levine soon persuaded him to cooperate and he provided information on Boesky's misdeeds. The SEC then turned to Boesky, who also decided to cooperate, fingering Michael Milken and even going so far as to wear a wire at a meeting with Milken in an effort to implicate him in the insider dealing scandal. Milken was eventually convicted of relatively minor reporting violations, but not of insider dealing. Boesky and Levine both received relatively short jail terms but massive fines for insider dealing.

The reason why these insider dealing revelations were so shocking in the 1980s was they were associated with the excitement and innovation in a rapidly expanding financial world. In the 1980s investors wanted action in the markets, and the merger and acquisitions mania was the way to get it. It was also the idea that people central to the M&A action – investment bankers abusing confidential information, institutional dealers who pig-gybacked on insider trades – were abusing their positions of trust, and a hero of the M&A game, Ivan Boesky, who had so publicly preached a phi-losophy of 'greed is good' in the mergers world, had turned out to be an insider dealer. The SEC had confirmed itself as an effective, perhaps even over-enthusiastic, enforcer of stock market regulations.

Back in the 1960s and 1970s, however, the investment world had more of a Wild West tinge than it does today. The US was by far and away the most modern and prosperous of the major economies, and western Europe was only just beginning to get back on its feet. One colourful US entrepre-neur, Bernie Cornfeld, built up a vast offshore mutual fund sales company, initially to draw upon the savings of the thousands of American expats and servicemen working in Europe after the Second World War, but it later attracted many investors from Europe and Latin America who, at that time, had few attractive investment opportunities and were suffering from draconian rules on moving funds abroad. Capital controls, which means governments preventing their citizens from moving their money abroad, were a major, and very frustrating, barrier to prosperity for businesspeo-ple in the 1960s – at one point British subjects (not 'citizens' until 1983) were forbidden from taking more than £50 abroad, which made it virtu-ally impossible even to go on a foreign holiday, let alone buy US shares directly. By the 1960s Cornfeld controlled a number of mutual funds from Switzerland, including what may have been the first 'fund of funds' (a fund that exclusively invests in other funds). Cornfeld served 11 months in a Swiss prison on fraud charges relating to a share issue of one of his funds, but was eventually acquitted; the vast sums of cash he controlled, however, attracted an even hungrier predator: Robert Vesco.

Robert Vesco

Robert Vesco was an Italian American, the son of a Detroit car worker. In the early 1960s Vesco had used borrowed money to acquire a series of car industry manufacturing units cobbled together into a conglomerate called the International Controls Corporation (ICC). In 1971, with Cornfeld in trouble, Vesco succeeded in a hostile takeover of Cornfeld's Investors Overseas Service (IOS). Most of IOS's assets were held in four funds with a total value of over $400 million, and were mainly invested in US securities. IOS was in trouble and needed cash, and Vesco, through his firm ICC, which was listed on the American Stock Exchange, loaned IOS money to keep going, In return, Vesco was able to purchase 45% of IOS preferred shares and 28% of its ordinary shares during 1971, and was voted in as chairman of the IOS board.

IOS, with its large sums of investors' money invested in blue chip US companies, looked like a cash cow to Vesco, who – allegedly – promptly began transferring money out of the blue chip firms and into various off-shore schemes he controlled. In October, IOS's main banking business was transferred to a new corporation based in the Bahamas. In December, IOS's real estate and insurance assets were transferred to another Bahamas company controlled by Vesco. Many of IOS's investors were known to have invested money illegally (by violating their own countries' capital controls and tax and investment laws, which at that time were strict) and it was thought that as much as $150 million in the funds would not be redeemed by such investors.

In the following year, Vesco took a new tack, attempting in a series of complex manoeuvres involving interrelated firms, many of them shells, to separate IOS funds from ICC, and to alter the funds' classification so that it would be hard for investors to get their money out, while continuing to retain ultimate control of the funds. At almost every turn, lawyers and officials involved in the process advised Vesco that what he proposed was unethical and failing in IOS's fiduciary duties to the original investors, most of whom were not wealthy; Vesco seems to have ignored them.

This activity, along with Vesco's lavish lifestyle, which included a private jet complete with sauna and disco, attracted the attention of the SEC.

Unlike the incompetence and bureaucratic mishandling that has characterised the SEC's recent investigations, the SEC of the early 1970s acted vigorously, accusing Vesco of having embezzled more than $200 million of investors' money. The dirty politics of the Nixon era was in evidence later, however, when G. Bradford Cook, the Chairman of the SEC, was forced to resign after it was discovered that he had ordered, at the behest of Nixon cronies, the removal from the SEC complaints against Vesco of any reference to Vesco's illegal $200,000 contribution to Nixon's campaign fund. This amount, it was alleged, was an attempt to bribe the Nixon administration to get the SEC off Vesco's back.

> Unlike the incompetence and bureaucratic mishandling that has characterised the SEC's recent investigations, the SEC of the early 1970s acted vigorously, accusing Vesco of having embezzled more than $200 million of investors' money.

The story now begins to take on a tawdry glamour, becoming like a kind of movie version of how slippery financiers are supposed to behave. By 1973, things were getting too hot for Vesco in the US. He told his pilot that 'from now on we'll be operating in the Caribbean and Central and South America. They're breaking my balls here in the US. I don't have to stand for that kind of shit.' In February Vesco fled to Costa Rica, continuing his legal battle with the US authorities. His company, ICC, was put under court supervision and had its shares suspended from stock market trading.

Then, as now, there were a number of violently anti-US regimes in Latin America. However, the centre-left government of José Figueres in tiny Costa Rica was not one of them. Figueres was a constructive reformer who, while willing to cooperate with the US in some areas, was determined to improve the country's economy. Vesco seems to have offered him a deal: investment in Costa Rica in return for some measure of protection against the US. The first investment was $2.15 million into Sociedad Agricola Industrial San Cristobal, an agricultural firm founded by Figueres that was a major employer in the country. Other investments followed, especially in high tech, as Vesco established himself in style, acquiring large estates and ranches, a fleet of vehicles and a small army of body-guards, and did his best to win over Costa Rican opinion by spreading the money around. Bizarre stories began to emerge that Vesco was building a movie-villain stronghold in the country, even equipping his 54-foot yacht with souped-up engines, state-of-the-art navigation systems and mounted machine guns. In 1974 two US businessmen testified to a Senate hearing that they had met Vesco to discuss the possibility of building a machine-gun factory in Costa Rica. One stated he had been told by Figueres's son that the factory would supply the Costa Rican army – quite plausible, per-haps, except for the fact Figueres had famously abolished the Costa Rican army permanently in the 1940s.

Although Vesco quickly became a household name and also the man whom numerous loony revolutionary schemers around the world claimed, probably falsely, was aiding them, it is still unclear why the US was unable to extradite him. There was an attempt in 1973 that failed when a Costa Rican judged ruled the fraud charges against Vesco were not covered by the extra-dition treaty – this is in fact common in extradition treaties – and another US application to extradite Vesco from the Bahamas, where Vesco also owned property, failed for the same reason. It is true that in March 1973 the Costa Rican parliament had passed a law banning the extradition of any foreigner on the basis of a simple request from a foreign country – known as 'the Vesco law'. This was seen widely as having been intended to protect Vesco specifically and prompted a riot of 2000 students in the Costa Rican capital. Nevertheless, the two extradition attempts, in Costa Rica and the Bahamas, had been refused on perfectly legitimate grounds.

So, was the US government not really trying to get Vesco? The Chairman of the relevant US Senate subcommittee, Senator Henry Jackson, certainly complained that the extradition efforts had been 'half-hearted attempts'. Costa Rica's new President, Oduber, also remarked that the extradition request seemed to have been intended to fail. The suspicion was that the Nixon administration was not overly keen to have Vesco back in the country just when the Watergate scandal had erupted – especially given that the money Vesco illegally contributed to Nixon allegedly went to pay for the Watergate operation. Further fuelling suspicion was the curious fact that Richard Nixon's nephew, Don, was working in Costa Rica as Vesco's personal assistant.

In 1974 *People* magazine depicted a dreary scene chez Vesco in Costa Rica, with his wife and four children edgy and uncomfortable in their walled mansion, surrounded by luxury but unsure of their future. Although Vesco was making an impact as a plutocratic benefactor in the region, he certainly does not seem to have thought of himself as untouchable, given his elaborate security arrangements. Vesco mounted a PR campaign, giving interviews for the US media from Costa Rica, and buying time on Costa Rican television, to proclaim his innocence. Nixon resigned as US President in August, and his successor, Gerald Ford, pardoned him; according to Vesco, general outrage at Nixon's pardon made it impossible for him, Vesco, also to receive a pardon from Ford as he had been promised.

Life in Costa Rica was not easy or cheap for Vesco, still only in his late thirties, and it was said to be costing him $500,000 a year. There were stories that the US had sent assassins to kill him. He had to pay off as many people as possible in the country, without having any discernible effect on his increasing unpopularity; his aircraft were getting seized by US creditors; the new President, Oduber, seemed less sympathetic towards him than Figueres had been; and some IOS investors had had the temerity to sue him in Costa Rica for the return of their money. If he could stay in the country for five years, he would be eligible for citizenship, which might provide some protection from the US authorities – he was still determined to stay out of the US. Then, in 1977, President Oduber was worried about getting re-elected, especially after major scandals revealed not only that Vesco's money had indirectly helped him to win his first presidential term, but also Vesco's companies had made fortunes during Costa Rica's 1975 privatisation of its oil and gas sector. Evidently Figueres' protection could no longer save Vesco, and Oduber asked him to leave the country – a move likely to prove hugely popular in a country that had come to detest Vesco, who, after failing to obtain Costa Rican citizenship amid wild protests and demonstrations, finally left the country in April 1978.

In the US, Jimmy Carter was now President, and his administration said that they still wanted to get Vesco. Vesco had other plans; three businessmen from Georgia, Carter's home state, had offered to try to smooth things over with the US government. If Vesco could get out of his problems with the US, he believed that he might be very useful in helping to conclude the Panama Canal Treaty, which was then being proposed. Meanwhile, Vesco's appetite for wild international schemes continued – it was essential to his modus operandi to generate a multitude of deals and try to play them off against each other. In 1979, newspaper reports appeared claiming that Vesco had visited Colonel Gaddafi in Libya several times in pursuit of an arms deal and that he had tried to arrange commissions to be paid by Libya to President Carter's unstable brother, Billy, who was also trying to do business with Gaddafi. It was also claimed that Vesco was attempting to arrange the release of eight transport planes Libya had purchased from Lockheed, but the US government had blocked; his commission on this deal was said to be worth $5 million. The 'Billygate' scandal was made much of at the time, and it was certainly suspected by many that Vesco had been trying to get at the White House through the President's incompetent brother; Jimmy Carter, however, was no fool, and it is quite clear that he did not allow Billy to have any improper influence over government policy. This sheds some light on Vesco's mentality. He seems to have been most at home with corrupt businessmen and shady politicos, and to have completely misread the likely behaviour of the Carter administration.

Vesco moved to Antigua in 1981, where he attempted to purchase part of the island of Barbuda with the help of politician Lester Bird, later to become prime minister. It is alleged that Vesco was able to obtain an Antiguan passport in a different name, and the Bird family assisted him in trying to set up an independent state on Barbuda. Discovering his presence in Antigua, the US instituted extradition proceedings. Vesco had to move on quickly. Trying to set up your own country is a very bad idea, unless you have powerful forces behind you, and Vesco didn't; he was losing his grip. He moved to Nicaragua, then ruled by a strongly anti-American regime, and got involved in drug smuggling to the US with Colombian, Nicaraguan and Cuban involvement (many Latin American revolutionaries supported drug smuggling as a way of attacking US society from the inside).

The decline was palpable. Soon there was nowhere for Vesco to go, except for the one great thorn in America's side: Castro's Cuba. It has been claimed that Vesco bribed Castro for permission to stay in Cuba, but this seems unlikely or, at least, unnecessary: Vesco, as a highly visible annoyance to the US, was clearly politically useful to Castro. He was also ideologically acceptable – as Castro told one interviewer, 'If he wants to live, let him live here. We don't care what he did in the United States.' Life in Cuba, however, was no paradise. Much of the money had leaked away, and, although living well by Cuban standards, Vesco's lifestyle had taken a substantial turn for the worse. Most of the planes, boats and bodyguards were gone and, by the 1990s, Vesco was living in a modest house far from the beach, surviving on whatever deals he could cobble together – but perhaps part of this humility was just a front to please the communist Cubans.

Then, out of the blue, Don Nixon, Richard Nixon's nephew, who had been Vesco's gopher in Costa Rica, made contact. 'Don Don', as he is nicknamed, claimed to have found a miracle drug, Trioxidal, that had cured his wife of arthritis and cancer, and couldn't get the backing of drug companies to conduct clinical trials in the US. Could Vesco help him arrange them to be done in Cuba? This was not a completely mad idea; under Castro, Cuba had during the 1980s put a lot of resources into trying to become a biotech powerhouse and the collapse of the USSR in 1991 only added to the economic incentives for making the Cuban industry work. Indeed, Cuba had even had some successes, for example the development of the first vaccine for meningitis B by Concepcion Campa Huergo, who first tested it on herself and her children.

Vesco and his hero-worshipping assistant 'Don Don', described by one commentator as having 'the demeanor of a hyperactive teenager', went into the drug development business in Cuba. It was not a success. In 1995 Vesco was arrested and put on trial on a range of charges that were eventually whittled down to fraud relating to Trioxidal. According to some reports, this was just an excuse – Vesco had broken too many rules during his time in Cuba, and the authorities had become tired of him. Another version has it that, following the end of the Cold War and the tidal wave of US businesspeople trying to do deals with Cuba, Castro no longer had any need of Vesco as a middleman, and Castro had never actually trusted him. Yet another alleges that Vesco was shopped to the Cuban authorities by a partner, Enrico Garzaroli, who had discovered Vesco did not have permission from the Cubans to operate. Whatever the truth of these stories, it is certain that Vesco was sentenced to 13 years in prison by a Cuban court in 1996; footage of his appearance in court shows a gaunt and haggard figure, a shadow of his former self. He was released in 2005 and died two years later of lung cancer.

Plus ça change ...

We, the investing public, need to have confidence in the markets. If we are naïve, we may believe that all investment business is properly run all of the time. If we are hopelessly paranoiac, we may believe that all investment business is crooked all of the time. Neither of these extremes are true, of course, but the fact remains that the financial services industry attracts more than its share of amoral greedy people, in the same way that show business attracts a disproportionate number of inordinately vain people. Knowing that there will always be some crooks, we need investor protection and anti-fraud measures on top of the main burden of regulation, which is to maintain orderly markets.

The aim of this chapter has been to explore two cases of high-level financial chicanery during two distinct periods in the past, during which the investment environment was very different from what it is today, and to show how difficult it can be to prevent or rectify such issues.

During the M&A boom of the 1980s, people who were excited by the stock market wanted to believe that there was nothing wrong with leveraged buyouts (buying companies with debt secured on the target company's own assets) even though wiser heads warned many of these companies might eventually collapse under the burden of excessive debt, as indeed eventually occurred. But stock market bulls (people who think

prices are going to go up) were more interested in the purported brilliance
of people like Michael Milken, who found a new way of financing these
deals, of Ivan Boesky, who made money jumping in and out of the companies that were 'in play', and of Drexel Burnham Lambert, the investment
bank that drove the M&A process in the 1980s. Milken was disgraced,
probably justifiably; Ivan Boesky was fined and jailed, entirely justifiably as
he had made much of his money by cheating through insider dealing; and
Drexel was put out of business after pleading no contest to a range of stock
manipulation charges. Dennis Levine was essentially a small fish practising
a rather obvious form of cheating, as the other financial professionals who
piggybacked on his transactions clearly recognised. It was not, in the 1980s,
terribly brilliant for Levine to try to hide his transactions by putting them
through foreign banks, because the very impetus that had created the environment for an M&A boom in the 1980s – financial de-regulation – also
made it much harder for foreign banks to resist US pressure to reveal the
identities of their clients. The US markets were where the action was and,
from a foreign bank's point of view, giving up one naughty client was pref-
erable to being forced to withdraw from the US markets.

Banking secrecy, which these days is a busted flush, was much more of
a reality in the 1960s and 1970s when the Cold War was in full swing, providing a strong demand for official and semi-official banking secrecy from
both sides of the Iron Curtain. Bernie Cornfeld exploited this banking
secrecy, and the fault lines between regulatory regimes in different countries. His firm, IOS, became a very large organisation, employing thousands
of salespeople, and operating its own mutual funds as well as investing in
funds owned by others. By the late 1960s it was heading for trouble as the
stock markets started to drop after a long bull run. The mishandling of the
money raised by an IOS public offering in Canada, driven by pressure from
the sales force that had been given shares in the firm, led to cash shortages.
The problems of an unorthodox commission system based on investment
returns, rather than on the sums invested, were revealed by 1970, when it
emerged that returns in 1969 had been much lower than predicted. IOS
might have staggered on for years, but, as Richard M. Meyer, a mutual
fund lawyer, has commented, Cornfeld 'only looks good when you

compare him to his successor, Robert Vesco. He championed taking a buck from anybody, without scruples.'

The extraordinary swoop on IOS made by Robert Vesco really was one of the major embezzlements of all time. It is unlikely that he could have done it today, at least in Europe or the US, given the better transparency, regulatory oversight and investor protection schemes that are now in place. It is difficult to see how Vesco thought he was going to get away with the scam unless one considers his age and personality. In 1971, the year he got control of IOS, he was only 35, a rip-roaring wheeler-dealer from a blue-collar background, on the make and in a hurry, running a ramshackle, debt-ridden conglomerate, ICC, by the seat of his pants.

Looting IOS might have been a great way to save ICC, but Vesco, according to the SEC, took a vast chunk of the money for himself. We don't know his motives; given his amazing capacity for rapid, big-time deals, it may merely have been that he thought he would be able to wriggle out of any SEC investigation. His relationship with the Nixon administration is not well understood – the only things we know for certain are that he did make an improper contribution to the gloriously named CREEP (Campaign to Re-elect the President), and he employed Nixon's nephew. A 1972 story in the *Washington Post* claimed that a key Nixon aide, John Erlichman, had warned 'Don Don' at length not to do anything to embarrass the President when he went to work for Vesco. A number of CIA memos from 1973 refer to a 'Research Project on Robert L. Vesco' and show an interest in IOS. It is possible that the connection is rather less sinister than meets the eye: what may have seemed to be a definite bribe to Vesco may have seemed to the Nixon team to be only a vague promise to see if anything could be done about Vesco's situation as an important international businessman with a little legal difficulty back home. Vesco was not politically sophisticated, as his subsequent relationships with Latin American politicians were to show.

> Looting IOS might have been a great way to save ICC, but Vesco, according to the SEC, took a vast chunk of the money for himself.

In the next chapter we will look in detail at two types of fraud that you are likely to encounter as an investor: Ponzi schemes and Pump and Dump operations.

3

Shiny new inventions and old tricks

Ponzi and 'Pump and Dump' schemes

We share the shock and dismay of our shareholders and others that the gold we thought we had at Busang now appears not to be there.

David Walsh, founder of the Bre-X mining company

Suppose you are hard up, but you live in a fairly prosperous community. You have an idea for improving the sales of your small, unprofitable business by buying a widget machine. A kind friend (Friend 1) lends you £10,000, telling you that he is not in a hurry to get it back. You rush home, delighted. Then it hits you: £10,000 seemed like a lot when you didn't have it, but now that you do have it, it doesn't seem quite enough.

You meet another friend, Friend 2, and casually mention how well the business is going (it isn't) and that Friend 1 has just invested £10,000. Friend 2's ears prick up. 'What kind of a return are we talking about?' she asks. You think quickly: deposit rates are about 4%, but the stock market is on a long-term slide ... what number should you tell her? Eventually you blurt out '10%'. Friend 2 looks at you narrowly. '10%? That seems awfully low.' You don't argue. You nod humbly. 'Well yes,' you say, 'As an astute investor you may be able to find better deals elsewhere. I am just trying to give a realistic assessment of the potential returns on this project. I don't want to disappoint anybody.'

A few days later Friend 2 contacts you. Now she seems to think that a 10% return isn't so bad after all, and she wants in. With a big display of reluctance, you accept her investment of £15,000. You need to think. A few days ago you had nothing, now you have £25,000. That's enough to buy a widget-making machine and pay for the company overheads for six months. Perhaps you should get to work. You start negotiating with manufacturers of widget machines.

Friend 3 calls you. He's heard exciting things about your business from Friend 2. Can he invest, too? Well, you think to yourself, you could always use some more money. You take an investment of £5,000. Now you have £30,000. You buy a new car and new clothes. You have £12,000 left.

You are in the kitchen, telling Friend 2 about how your business is going. You're carried away and start to exaggerate. You tell her that sales have shot up, and the money is pouring in. 'Oh good,' says Friend 2, 'How about a distribution of profits?' You write her a cheque for £1,500. As you are doing this, Friend 1 passes by and asks what is going on? Friend 2 tells him; so now you have to give Friend 1 £1,000 as his share of the profits.

But there have been no profits. You haven't even bought the widget machine that is supposed to be generating these profits. You have £9,500 left. You had better buy a widget machine pronto and start production. Then Friend 3 telephones you, very apologetically – he needs his £5,000 back immediately. He isn't worried about any profits, he says, he just wants the money back right now. You post him a cheque for £5,000. You have £4,500 left. That's not enough to buy a widget machine. You had better get some new investors ...

Variations on the story above, the plot of a hundred plays and novels, occur often enough in real life, especially in closely linked communities where people are more likely to trust one another. Informal deals are struck, often on the basis of insufficient information, but the investors rely on the investment promoter's sense of obligation to community members

– 'he is one of us, he can't cheat me' – to ensure that they get their money back. Exploiting communal ties of this kind, incidentally, is known as 'affinity fraud'. Investors who would never invest money so informally with a stranger are often willing to trust a member of their own community, with whom they feel they will continue to have close contact.

You, the investment promoter in the story, did not start out with a carefully worked out plan to defraud anyone. A succession of bad decisions has put you in a predicament: either you go on getting more money from new investors, so that you can pay out returns and withdrawals to earlier investors, or the money will run out. Tempted by the prospect of receiving further investments, you misrepresented the prospects for the business and then spent a large proportion of the funds on things that made you look better, but did nothing to progress the widget machine project. Now you are going to have to maintain the lie and draw in even more investors, even if you sincerely intend to make the widget machine business work. In other words, you may not have begun with the intention of committing fraud, but you are now having to manage an elaborate deception on an ongoing basis.

The investors themselves have, of course, been negligent. They have not done their 'due diligence': they have not required a formal agreement covering all eventualities, they haven't asked for any real detail about the proposed investment or the existing business, and they haven't tried to verify independently any of the claims you have made to them. They have relied on the information that you have given them. They have been happy to receive the returns you have paid out to them because they believed your false statement that these sums were taken from the profits created by the business. The fraud described above is a hardy perennial, well known in the nineteenth century, and alleged by the SEC to have been the fundamental principle involved in the recent Bernard Madoff and Allen Stanford scandals in the 'noughties'. It is known as a 'Ponzi scheme' after a case in the US in 1920 when Charles Ponzi operated a business that was supposed to be making profits by buying international postal reply coupons cheaply abroad and redeeming them at a profit in the United States.

Although the business was actually running at a loss, he attracted a large number of investors by promising inordinately high returns, and paying earlier investors returns not out of profits, but out of investment monies provided by new investors – this is the key feature of a Ponzi scheme. Ponzi schemes are destined to collapse because eventually it will become impossible to obtain new investment money to cover payments out. This may occur during a market downturn, for example, when many investors suddenly want to take money out of the market. Ponzi schemes are frequently private deals, but appear at almost every level of business, from the smallest to the largest, and can sometimes be maintained for years before they collapse. Every year, the regulators in the US and UK prosecute a number of Ponzi schemes, many of which do not receive much publicity. The Madoff and Stanford schemes are well known because of the staggering scale of the fraud – lesser Ponzi schemes affecting fewer people tend not to attract much attention. Madoff's operation, however, is particularly interesting because of some clever features of the scheme, and is discussed in some detail below. First, however, we should consider another common form of market fraud, called in the US 'Pump and Dump'.

> Although the business was actually running at a loss, he attracted a large number of investors by promising inordinately high returns, and paying earlier investors returns not out of profits, but out of investment monies provided by new investors – this is the key feature of a Ponzi scheme.

'Pump and Dump' can refer generally to any type of fraudulent operation that involves persuading investors the shares of a certain company, often a small one in an obscure sector or market, are rising, in order to sell shares the fraudster bought earlier at a higher price. More narrowly, it may refer only to organisations that specialise in hard-selling a series of such companies to investors by media stories, telemarketing and internet campaigns. One of the largest cases of the former type was Bre-X Minerals, a Canadian mining company.

Bre-X was formed in 1989 by David Walsh and was based in Calgary, Alberta in Canada. It was listed on the small Alberta stock exchange but was largely inactive until 1993 when a geologist, John Felderhof, recommended a number of mineral deposit rights for sale in the Pacific Rim. Bre-X then employed Felderhof to manage the exploration of a site at Busang, in the Indonesian part of Borneo. During the exploration one of the team, a geologist named Michael de Guzman, reported that there might be as much as two million ounces of gold at Busang. Exploratory drilling at Busang continued, and soon there were estimates that the land held 30 million ounces of gold. Not surprisingly Bre-X's share price began to go up, rising from a few pennies to over $14 by mid-1995. In April of the following year Bre-X was listed on the larger Toronto stock exchange, and the share price hit $280.

With analysts' estimates of the value of the Busang find now going as high as 200 million ounces, other players wanted in on the deal. Indonesia was then ruled by President Suharto, who presided over a notoriously corrupt regime in which most of the profits obtained by exploiting the country's immense natural resources were in the hands of members of Suharto's own family and a small elite of cronies. Bre-X was forced to accept that they would have to share the find with some unwelcome partners. Eventually these partners turned out to be a large Canadian mining company Barrick Gold, who were linked with Tutut, one of Suharto's daughters, and a US firm, Freeport-McMoRan Copper & Gold, which was associated with Bob Hasan, one of Suharto's main business cronies. Bre-X had to agree to allow Freeport to operate the mine.

Freeport then took over and began to perform its own due diligence, drilling at Busang to verify Bre-X's findings. Its initial reports were positive but by spring 1997 there was a problem: Bre-X's samples had been found to contain 4.4 grams of gold per tonne, while Freeport's samples, taken nearby, only contained 0.01 grams.

Freeport wanted an explanation. On 19 March David de Guzman, the Filipino geologist who had made the original findings, was flown by helicopter across the jungle to Busang. He never arrived. According to the pilot, de Guzman had jumped out of the aircraft of his own accord. It was widely believed at the time that de Guzman had been pushed out by Suharto's men; subsequently, one of de Guzman's widows has claimed that he is still alive. Whatever the truth of that matter, the cat was now out of the bag. Within a week Freeport announced that it had only found negligible amounts of gold in its samples, and, significantly, there were 'visual differences' between the flecks of gold in the Bre-X samples and those in the Freeport samples, which suggested one set of samples might have been 'salted'. Bre-X announced that it was hiring an independent firm, Strathcona, to undertake further tests. In the meantime, shares in Bre-X were suspended.

Strathcona produced its report in May, which supported Freeport's findings and stated that Bre-X's samples had been interfered with. 'Salting' samples is a perennial hazard in the mining industry, and elaborate measures are taken to detect the practice. In the case of Bre-X, it is alleged that tens of thousands of mineral samples had been tampered with over a period of three-and-a-half years. Bre-X's share price continued its downward trajectory on Strathcona's news, and the company, which at the height of the excitement had had a market capitalisation of $6 billion, eventually went bankrupt. Bre-X's founder, David Walsh, died in 2008, and a prosecution of John Felderhof in Canada ended in his acquittal, leaving the unfortunate Bre-X investors with no definitive explanation of who had engineered the fraud.

These investors had included established financial organisations such as Fidelity Investments and Quebec's pension fund as well as a host of ordinary investors. The fact that Bre-X had been put in the TSE index after it was listed on the Toronto Stock Exchange (TSE) had made it much more 'investable' for funds that were looking for performance comparable to an index. According to Fidelity, who would not comment on the performance of its individual investments, overall its portfolio was up during the period in which it held some Bre-X shares – in other words, it had spread the risk across a range of investments, thereby reducing the damage from a bad loss on any single investment.

Bre-X had jumped through a series of regulatory hoops, both in Canada and the US, to satisfy the authorities that it had found gold. Although several of the principals involved did very well out of Bre-X, selling millions of dollars worth of shares before the price collapsed, no one went to jail. No compensation was paid. It was, perhaps, the perfect crime – we don't even know for certain who committed it.

If you are the kind of investor who likes to dabble in high-risk/high-reward companies in lesser markets, you have to face up to the facts that, first, you cannot foretell the future and, second, some of your investments may incur heavy losses. Encountering a situation like Bre-X, you have to recognise the possibility, however remote, of fraud. Given these facts, it is foolhardy and amateurish to bet your entire portfolio on the outcome. Spreading the risk is the best defence against 'Pump and Dump' operations; it won't prevent a loss on a given investment, but it will reduce the damage the loss causes you, allowing you to live on to fight another day.

Naïve investors often hope to make money fast by investing in a series of single, high-risk companies, often listed on obscure stock markets. There is a thriving newsletter industry that lives on such investors, generating endless 'buy' recommendations for such stocks. The truth is that most of these optimistic gamblers will lose money overall, but this does not prevent new people coming to the market every year with the same old naïve expectations.

So, if you are the kind of person who can't resist taking a punt on some hot new company, just remember that someone may be running a 'Pump and Dump' scam, and don't bet more than you are prepared to lose. Most people are not reckless gamblers, and are therefore less vulnerable to 'Pump and Dump' schemes. They are, however, very vulnerable to Ponzi schemes, especially if these schemes are dressed up as sound, conservative schemes that produce steady, modest returns, as was the case in the Madoff and Stanford affairs. Such investors rely heavily on the regulatory system to protect them and this led to an outcry when it emerged the SEC had been warned repeatedly something was wrong with Madoff's operation

> So, if you are the kind of person who can't resist taking a punt on some hot new company, just remember that someone may be running a 'Pump and Dump' scam, and don't bet more than you are prepared to lose.

but had failed to act. The SEC had been a ruthless enforcer in the 1970s and 1980s, but by the time of the Madoff revelations, the SEC had become a much less capable organisation. We will now look in more detail at how Madoff was able to run his scheme for so long.

The SEC and Bernard Madoff

Early on in his career, Madoff had been given office space in Manhattan by his father-in-law, Saul Alpern, an accountant, who also lent him $50,000 to invest. Soon after, Carl Shapiro, a rich businessman, gave him a further $100,000 to invest. Madoff used this money to trade actively, and the commissions he earned subsidised his small penny share broking business. He encouraged Alpern to bring him more customers, in return for a fee, and soon his client base exceeded the exemption then allowed by the SEC to small investment managers (managers with 15 or fewer clients did not have to obtain an SEC licence). In 1962 Madoff asked Alpern to merge many of the small investors he was finding into one account so that it would seem he still qualified for the SEC licence exemption, and shortly after Alpern merged his accountancy firm into Madoff's, and brought in the accountant Frank Avellino to help find more investors.

Thus Frank Avellino became one of the first and longest-serving agents to 'feed' Madoff with new investors. This is of interest because his firm, Avellino & Bienes, was the subject of the first known Madoff-related complaint to the SEC, in 1991. This complaint illustrates a problem that many investors encounter from time to time: exaggerated assurances of safety. Two private investors with Avellino & Bienes provided the SEC with sales material from that firm, which should have set anyone's alarm bells ringing. In a letter of 7 August 1991 from Avellino & Bienes, a potential customer was told that:

'Avellino & Bienes invests with one particular Wall Street Broker (the same company since we first started doing business over 25 years ago) who buys and sells stocks and bonds in the name of Avellino & Bienes ... We do not encourage new accounts and therefore we do not solicit same. We do, however, like to accommodate those individuals, etc. that are recommended as you have been ... Summarily, this is a very private group and no financial statements, prospectuses or brochures have been printed or are available ... The money that is sent to A&B is a loan to A&B who in turn invests it on behalf of A&B for which our clients receive quarterly interest payments ... Interest rate is 16.0% annually.'

On the face of it, then, the deal was attractive – a loan to the firm in return for a healthy interest rate. What should always alarm an investor, especially a small one, though, is the claim to exclusivity and privacy; the fact is that investment managers will usually take anyone's money, especially if, as in this case, the minimum investment was a low $5,000.

The SEC was also given a fact sheet produced by an investment adviser who was bringing new clients to Avellino & Bienes. This document asserted 'Is it safe? Yes. 100%. At no time is a trade made that puts your money at risk. In over 20 years there has never been a losing transaction' and went on to explain 'all of these funds are send [sic] to a New York broker who invests same on behalf of Avellino & Bienes. The underlying trades, made for the account of Avellino & Bienes are, in general, made as simultaneous purchases of convertible securities and its short sale of the common stock, locking in a profit. Other forms of riskless trading are also used.' These claims are the real give-away. Risk-free trading for 20 years? It's as illusory as the philosopher's stone sought by the mediaeval alchemists. As an investor, you owe it to yourself to understand exactly how it is being done, not just take someone's word for it.

When they investigated, SEC staff reported that it seemed the firm had been 'engaged in selling securities to the public, which are unregistered, in violation of Section 5(a) of the Securities Act of 1933' and expressed concern about 'the lack of transparency about how the monies were invested' and the possibility the firm was running a Ponzi scheme. When the firm's bosses, Frank Avellino and Michael Bienes, were brought in to explain themselves in July 1992 they stated that they had invested $400 million of investors' money with Madoff along with a further $40 million of their own money, and described Madoff's trading strategy as a series of complex hedges using puts and calls on major stocks, a 'split-strike conversion strategy'.

Later that year an SEC team conducted a 'brief' examination of Madoff's firm, principally to establish whether the trading positions reported by Avellino and Bienes were genuine. The investigators were not told that they were investigating a Ponzi scheme, and in any case the focus was on Avellino and Bienes, not on Madoff, and any documents

Madoff provided were simply assumed to be accurate. Madoff's paper-work appeared to confirm Avellino and Bienes's story, and no check was made on where Madoff obtained the money to make payments to them. Investigators admitted at a later inquiry that they were aware of Madoff's prominence in the industry and his good reputation made them feel there was no need to investigate his firm more thoroughly.

In November, the SEC filed a complaint against Avellino & Bienes for unlawfully selling unregistered securities (i.e. the loans investors made to them) as an unregistered investment company. No suspicion of fraud was mentioned, and neither was Madoff's firm. The court appointed a receiver and trustee to liquidate Avellino & Bienes and to oversee the return of investors' money. According to Lee Richards, the Receiver and Trustee, his responsibility was to 'independently verify account balances on the records of Madoff, but not to independently verify that the securities Madoff were reporting actually existed. In other words, we'd go as far as Madoff's records, and as long as they were consistent with what we thought investors of Avellino & Bienes were owed and indeed we got the money and securities, then I think ... we had done our job.' The following year, despite the court-appointed auditors' complaints that they could not trace much of the firm's paperwork, most if not all of the investors' money was returned to them successfully, and the firm was fined $250,000, with its bosses, Avellino and Bienes, being personally fined a further $50,000 each and banned from selling unregistered securities in the future. According to one of the SEC's staff lawyers at the time, 'we were quite satisfied this was a very good result', especially as the investors had all got their money back.

It could be argued that, without the benefit of hindsight, the SEC was not entirely unreasonable in its attitude. The big fear in financial regulation is that the small private investors don't get all of their money back, as so often occurs in major financial scandals. Since they had no reason to suspect Madoff, the SEC appears to have assumed that all the misrepresentation and exaggeration had been done by Avellino & Bienes, and having made that assumption, could pat itself on the back for having nipped a problem-atic operation in the bud before investors lost any money. The investigation team was 'relatively inexperienced', according to the SEC, and although, as experts later pointed out, the fact that Avellino & Bienes had had such a very long relationship with Madoff should have stimulated the team to conduct closer checks on Madoff, it did not do so. At the time of writing it has not been established in this case whether or not Madoff did indeed provide phoney paperwork to the investigators or whether he repaid the money out of other investors' funds.

Further SEC investigations

In 2000 the analyst Harry Markopolos approached the SEC with evidence that Madoff might be committing fraud, setting off an unsuccessful process taking years of bureaucratic misunderstandings and delays, which are discussed later (see Chapter 9.) In May 2001 two articles appeared questioning Madoff's success, one in the obscure *MARHedge* trade journal entitled 'Madoff tops charts; skeptics ask how', and one in the better-known *Barron's* magazine entitled 'Don't Ask, Don't Tell'.

The *MARHedge* article stated that Madoff had $6–7 billion under management, which came mainly from three feeder funds, and reported that people were 'baffled by the way the firm has obtained such consistent, nonvolatile returns month after month and year after year', suggesting the complicated 'split-strike' options strategy Madoff claimed he was using to achieve these steady returns could not achieve such low volatility (here 'volatility' simply means the degree to which the returns vary in each period – normally in the stock market you would expect to see some variation in the returns over time).

The article provided much detail of Madoff's smooth and superficially plausible explanations for this anomaly, but when pressed for specifics he replied, 'I'm not interested in educating the world on our strategy, and I won't get into the nuances of how we manage risk.' The *Barron's* article was rather more dramatic in tone, claiming that Madoff's investor accounts 'have produced compound average annual returns of 15% for more than a decade' and reporting one investor as saying 'What Madoff told us was, "If you invest with me, you must never tell anyone that you're invested with me. It's no one's business what goes on here.'" Although neither article accused Madoff of dishonesty, both had homed in on the nub of the issue: no one – except Bernie and, perhaps, his assistants – could explain how the split-strike conversion strategy that he claimed to use could, in fact, produce the pattern of returns he had been generating for so many years. According to the later inquiry, no one in the SEC's North East Regional Office (which was responsible for Madoff) read either of these articles until years later.

In 2002 a different SEC department, the Office of Compliance Inspections and Examinations (OCIE) in Washington, DC, conducted an inspection of registered hedge funds, and in doing so asked hedge fund managers to report any suspicious activity that they might encounter. In early 2003 a hedge fund manager contacted an OCIE inspector with a detailed account of how, as part of their regular business, his firm had considered investing with Madoff's feeder funds but upon performing 'due diligence' (the process of thoroughly investigating an investment) they had uncovered some alarming inconsistencies. The most notable of these was when the manager and a colleague, an expert options trader, were told by Madoff at a meeting that he traded options for his split-strike conversion strategy through the Chicago Board of Options Exchange (CBOE). The options trader pounced, asking Madoff how this was possible, since not enough options were traded on the CBOE to make Madoff's strategy possible, given the huge amounts of money he was managing. The options trader subsequently telephoned former colleagues in the CBOE market 'and I asked them all if they were trading with Madoff. And nobody was. Nobody was doing these OEX options. And in fact, the funny part about it was they all said, yeah. You know, I hear that he's doing all these trades but, you know, we don't see it anywhere'. In making his report to the SEC, the hedge fund manager supplied substantial detail, and included the *MARHedge* article of the previous year.

The OCIE did not act quickly. In the autumn of 2003 the hedge fund manager's report was passed on to the OCIE's Self-Regulatory Organisations Group (SRO Group). It did nothing until December, when it received another tip about Madoff from another SEC department, misleadingly suggesting that Madoff was 'front-running' (illegally buying and selling securities in advance of customers' orders, a practice which the OCIE had already established could not account for Madoff's performance). The SRO Group contacted Madoff, who later stated 'it was readily apparent to him that they were focused on front-running and [he] thought it was part of a sweep that the SEC was doing on front-running'.

The picture of the SRO Group's investigation of Madoff that emerged in the SEC inquiry of 2009 is distressing to those of us who still have some faith in officialdom: the operation was bungled outrageously. Staff testified that the department was expanding by recruiting young people, and many in the department were inexperienced, had received no training, and were expected to learn on the job. Many were lawyers who knew nothing about financial securities. The SRO Group did not request the help of in-house investment experts at the SEC. A 'Planning Memorandum' for the investigation was drawn up in December that appeared to miss completely the possibility of Madoff not front-running, but committing a much more serious fraud. The official in charge of the investigation was asked why he had not thought to investigate other issues highlighted in the hedge fund manager's report of early 2003, which included the two points mentioned above – the strangely consistent performance of Madoff's investments and the fact that the volume of options traded in the market did not appear to be large enough to support a split-strike conversion strategy on the scale Madoff would have to be doing it, if it were true – and doubts about the genuine independence of Madoff's auditor. He replied that he did not remember seeing these points in the hedge fund manager's report. When asked why he focused on front-running, he replied that 'my group was responsible for trading exams, so we focused on, in essence, the trading aspect of the allegation. ... it could be mainly because that was the area of expertise for my crew.' Another official involved volunteered the information that he had focused on front-running because it 'was just a theory that seemed to make sense to me, you know. ... [M]y theory was, and I think I've since learned or come to understand that it's not a very good theory ... [was] it did seem likely to me that having access to that type of retail order flow could be valuable and that you could profitably trade ahead of it and make money' and later admitted 'I didn't know anything, very little anyway, about hedge funds and mutual funds and how they operated.'

Thus, a group of wet-behind-the-ears lawyers with little knowledge of the securities industry set out to investigate if Madoff had committed a particular kind of offence – front-running – that any expert would have told them could not account for the returns Madoff was paying his investors. They chose to ignore specific and plausible problem areas that had been clearly outlined in the hedge fund manager's report and the *MARHedge* article.

It gets worse. The team drafted a letter to NASD, a stock market in which Madoff was active, requesting all Madoff's trading data, but did not send it. According to the SEC inquiry, this was apparently because it was quicker to use the data that Madoff supplied, and also because it was the OCIE's habit to rely on data supplied by the firms it was investigating. Even in cases of suspected fraud! Nor did the team ask the firms bringing investors to Madoff for information about the feeder funds, as it had intended to do, according to its Planning Memorandum. When Madoff denied, early in 2004, that he was running a hedge fund, stating he was simply executing orders on behalf of institutional clients, no effort was made to verify these claims, even though they clearly contradicted the information given in the hedge fund manager's report of 2002. Members of the investigating team spoke to the hedge fund manager, who evidently explained everything all over again, but to no avail – the team went merrily on in pursuit of evidence of front-running. One member of staff testified at the inquiry, 'it's just crazy stuff that goes on in this office. It was weird. It was like a sitcom or something. It didn't exist in the real world ...'.

Nevertheless, the investigators gamely tried to get to grips with the split-strike conversion strategy, but had difficulty in making sense of the data Madoff had provided. They also began to wonder if Madoff was actually acting as an investment adviser, even though he claimed he wasn't. Then, suddenly, in April 2004, they were ordered to drop the Madoff investigation for the time being and concentrate on another priority, a claim that some broker–dealers were receiving, but not reporting, commissions from mutual fund companies as a reward for recommending certain mutual funds to their customers. In the same year, the SEC's North East Regional Office (NERO) began an investigation of Madoff without any knowledge of the SRO Group's investigation, which was only discovered when Madoff told them about it. NERO and the SRO Group communicated briefly about this, and the SRO Group sent NERO some files, but did not answer many of NERO's requests for information. External experts from FTI Consulting were brought in later to analyse the mess, and concluded that because of the SRO Group's avoidable foul-ups a good opportunity to discover Madoff's wrong-doing had been missed in 2004.

The NERO investigation had started when an SEC examiner, during a routine examination of the fund-managing firm Renaissance Technologies LLC in 2004, had found some internal correspondence questioning Madoff's operation, highlighting anomalies in Madoff's equity trading, his misrepresentation of his option trading, his unusual secrecy, the questionable independence of his auditor, his unusually steady returns and his unusual fee structure. Ignoring much of the evidence in this correspondence, the NERO team chose to focus on only two possible forms of fraud, front-running and 'cherry-picking'. Cherry-picking is the practice of performing transactions in the stock market and then deciding later which account to assign them to, depending on whether the result is profitable or not. The practice is illegal if it is not disclosed in advance to customers. These two fraudulent practices were bad choices for investigation, because it was unlikely that either of them could have produced sufficient profits to fund the returns that Madoff was giving to his investors. Also, the Renaissance correspondence had provided a very full analysis of why Madoff must have been misrepresenting the way he traded options (remember, Madoff always said that he made his money using a proprietary split-strike conversion strategy using options) – but the NERO team ignored this. As with the SRO Group, NERO did not use staff with the appropriate skills to conduct the investigation – instead of using experts on investment advisers, they used staff who were used to examining broker–dealers. Most of the material that NERO examined was provided by Madoff, and little effort was made to verify its accuracy with third parties

– if this had been done, Madoff's wrong-doing would have been revealed. NERO supervisors prevented investigators from pursuing various 'red flags' that came up during the investigation, and if they had done so they would have found Madoff had misrepresented many of the details of his operation to them. NERO's final report found that Madoff was not front-running, accused him of a few very minor technical violations, and entirely failed to address many potentially serious issues the investigators had uncovered. They seem to have got quite close on occasion – Madoff had been angry and unsettled during the investigation, quite unlike his normally smooth and friendly handling of the SEC.

Some frauds just never go away

Pump and Dump and Ponzi schemes are unlikely ever to disappear. They are like beautifully adapted parasites, with every organ delicately calibrated to take advantage of their hosts.

Pump and Dump schemes work because the stock markets are skewed towards optimism – most investors hope to make money by holding investments whose prices go up, not down, and they are thereby automatically vulnerable to plausible stories that a given investment is going to go up – but was the Bre-X story plausible? Well, geology is a real science – it appeared to investors that a host of geological experts and regulators had endorsed the gold find at Busang.

> **Pump and Dump and Ponzi schemes are unlikely ever to disappear. They are like beautifully adapted parasites**

In reality, however, Bre-X had raised most of its money in private placements, involving much lower regulatory standards than a public offering. It had only ever published one prospectus, in 1989 in Alberta, long before it claimed to have found the gold. The fact that Barrick and other large mining companies wanted to get in on the Busang deal encouraged investors to believe that the deal must be genuine. The listing of Bre-X on the Toronto market index also seemed to be an endorsement. When quizzed later, geologists and industry analysts claimed it had seemed impossible that the find could have been salted on such a large scale. None of this amounted to overwhelming proof that the gold existed, but an incautious investor might be forgiven for accepting this circumstantial evidence. And that's how this kind of fraud works: the deal is made to look real enough to attract the mugs. Nevertheless, rational investors should never be wiped out by a single Pump and Dump scheme, because rational investors do not put their entire portfolio into one tiny company listed on an obscure stock market, however attractive it may appear to be – they spread the risk across a range of investments.

Ponzi schemes, on the other hand, can be much more insidious, especially if they are designed to look as if they are conservative, stable investments. Although they are eventually doomed to failure, they can run on for years, and the fact that they pay returns regularly reassures existing investors. Ponzi schemes are skilfully tailored towards their target market: Madoff covered himself in respectability and conservatism to appeal to an affluent, fairly sophisticated clientele, but other schemes, in less sophisticated markets, are calibrated differently. For example, two large schemes in China required investors (mainly poor Chinese peasants) to feed 'special ants' in a box that would then be collected and ground up as an aphrodisiac – it's hard to imagine Madoff's victims finding the prospect of spraying sugar water on ants twice a day an exciting investment. A well-designed Ponzi scheme may be difficult for regulators to close down, even if they have suspicions. This makes them particularly dangerous to investors who rely on the regulators to protect them. In most cases, by the time the regulators act, it will be too late for many investors. Beware!

PART TWO

Let's go to work: the confidence men in action

4

Sharks or maniacs?

As things stand, we do not know the prevalence of psychopathy among those who work on Wall Street. It may be even higher than 10% ...

Robert Hare, leading researcher on psychopathology

There is nothing unusual about financial dishonesty. Just look around you; how many people of your acquaintance could you really trust with a substantial sum of money? We encounter petty dishonesty each day, from the crafty shopkeeper to the lying repairman. We all have a few false friends, dodgy relatives and crooked work colleagues. We all have to deal with large firms that use deceitful practices bordering on the illegal – remember all those pushy sales calls from utilities companies trying to get you to switch supplier, or to switch back? As we go through life we develop ways of handling these dreary, everyday baddies. We count our change, and are careful how we deal with the plumber and the roofer. We know that any money we lend to crazy cousin Jim isn't going to be paid back. We learn to assert our consumer rights when dealing with large firms. In other words, we know perfectly well that many people and organisations can't be trusted completely, and we cope.

However, society can't function without institutions and roles that have higher standards of financial integrity. We expect our solicitor not to pinch our money when we buy a house (it does happen, but very rarely). We expect our doctor not to kill us with an injection and then try to falsify our wills (but remember Harold Shipman?) We expect firms to not take more than they should when we make a purchase using a card (but it does occur). We expect our high street bank to run our accounts accurately (as happens most of the time). And when it comes to lower-risk, consumer-type investments, we expect the brokers, advisers, accountants and fund managers to operate honestly.

Trust, then, is an essential feature of our financial lives. Someone who is able to inspire trust in people is, if he or she is dishonest, in a good position to cheat us. If we look around us, we see that many people, perhaps even most people, are not very honest about money, and we know not to trust them with money – so what kind of person is able to inspire trust in us and then defraud us?

Perceptions of who is trustworthy vary enormously. One person's obviously corrupt barrow boy is another person's visionary financial genius. It seems likely that trust-inspiring fraudsters do not fit into a single personality type – and different types may prey on different types of victims. As investors we must be students of human nature, and in this chapter we will explore some of the psychological research into the personalities of fraudsters. Understanding what makes a fraudster tick is more difficult, and more ambiguous, than you might think. Most of the literature on fraudsters deals with their methods and how to detect them, rather than with the personalities of fraudsters, and there is little consensus among behavioural psychologists on how these should be defined and understood.

It seems clear that fraudsters' motives vary considerably – their motives can't all be explained away simply as a desire for more money. In this regard, trying to identify what specific fraudsters think that they need can be helpful. A need may be straightforward and quantifiable, such as 'I need to make back all the $50 million I lost on behalf of the company/clients', but even then the underlying motives may be complex. For example, it has been alleged that Sam Israel, founder of the Bayou hedge fund, had a deep need to prove to his extended family that he was becoming a financial success; the prospect of admitting that Bayou had started losing money from the outset, and in a bull market, seemed unimaginably humiliating. Such a powerful emotional need can easily overwhelm consideration of the risks of getting caught or drive spurious justifications, such as 'I am going to win the money back soon by making new investments', as appears to have occurred in Israel's case. This is a useful insight: we cannot automatically assume that fraudsters will calculate the consequences of their actions 'rationally', since they may be driven by personal issues that override any sober assessments they may make. Furthermore some of them may have severe personality disorders that drive them to make 'irrational' or 'short-sighted' decisions; they may, for example, be psychopaths.

Are some financial fraudsters psychopaths?

The short answer is that we don't know for certain. Research on psychopaths has primarily been focused on violent criminals, and researchers say that it is difficult to conduct adequate research (which is quite invasive) on psychopathy in the workplace. The concept of the psychopath first became popularised in the 1940s, following important work done by Hervey M. Cleckley, an American psychiatrist who devoted much of his life to studying the condition. Cleckley published a book, *The Mask of Sanity*, in 1941, which is widely regarded as a seminal work in the field. Confusion with the unrelated concept of psychosis, along with waves of alarmism in the popular media, has led some to doubt that the idea of the psychopath is valid, but extensive research during the last two decades has greatly improved the clinical understanding of psychopathy and methods for its diagnosis.

The idea of the psychopath is a scientific construct, a modern term that has been invented to describe a syndrome (a personality disorder involving a specific cluster of different personality traits and behaviours). Diagnosing a psychopath involves the administration of elaborate tests; it is not, therefore, possible to diagnose a historical figure as a psychopath or to diagnose a major fraudster, such as Madoff or Stanford, on the basis of their media coverage.

Nevertheless, there are good grounds for suspecting that a disproportionately large percentage of financial fraudsters may be psychopaths. For example, some of the classic characteristics of psychopaths, such as

> Nevertheless, there
> are good grounds for
> suspecting that
> a disproportionately large
> percentage of financial
> fraudsters may
> be psychopaths.

recklessness, charm, deceitfulness and the absence of feelings of empathy or guilt seem, on the face of it, to match many of the fraudsters discussed in this book. Furthermore, it is established that psychopaths are drawn to occupations in which they can abuse positions of trust, and as the financial services industry offers many positions of trust it would appear to be attractive to such individuals.

It is sometimes claimed that 10% of financial services workers are psychopaths. This is not supported by scientific evidence; in fact, there has been very little research into psychopathy in finance or, more broadly, in the corporate world in general. Studies of corporate psychopathy have generally used samples that are too small to be representative. One such study found that 4% of the corporate executives in their sample were psychopathic. Although this cannot be generalised to the wider population of all corporate executives, it is suggestive, since 4% is substantially higher than the 1% estimated for psychopathy in the general population.

While pointing out that there has been insufficient research into psychopathy in finance to answer the question definitively, Robert Hare, a leading authority on psychopaths, argues that the percentage of psychopaths on Wall Street 'may be even *higher* than 10%, on the assumption that psychopathic entrepreneurs and risk-takers tend to gravitate toward financial watering holes, particularly those that are enormously lucrative and poorly regulated. But, until the research has been conducted, we are left with anecdotal evidence and widespread speculation.'

So what are psychopaths really? Hare has memorably described them as 'intraspecies predators', in other words, animals that predate on their own kind. This predation can take numerous forms, not necessarily violent, and not all psychopaths commit crimes or end up in prison. The current understanding of the condition is that it is a matter of having less or more of certain qualities, rather than either having or not having these qualities. Diagnosis involves complex tests that measure scores in four 'domains' or areas of the personality. To meet the criteria for being a psychopath, you must score highly in these areas on the test, and these data must be cross-checked and supported by other information taken from, for example, medical and criminal records. In the well-known test, Psychopathy Checklist – Revised (PCL – R), an individual must score 30 out of 40 to be judged a psychopath.

The key features of the psychopathic personality are, according to Hare:

◆ glibness and superficiality
◆ egocentricity and grandiosity
◆ lack of remorse or guilt
◆ lack of empathy
◆ deceitfulness and manipulativeness
◆ shallow emotions.

These features lead to identifiable behaviours involving:

◆ impulsiveness
◆ poor behaviour controls
◆ a need for excitement
◆ a lack of responsibility
◆ antisocial behaviour.

Psychopaths are often superficially charming and extremely skilful at deception and manipulation. They choose their victims carefully, and have an uncanny ability to identify and exploit victims' psychological weaknesses. They have no sense of empathy and are indifferent to others except as objects to be used – psychopaths appear to be unable to imagine what it is like to be another person, but 'learn' to disguise this. They do not feel guilty for any crime they commit, however heinous. They have big ideas about who they are and what they expect to achieve, and often feel themselves to be above the law. They have a strong sense of entitlement and have contempt, which they conceal, for social norms.

Although psychopaths are formidable adversaries and extremely dangerous for their victims, they are by no means superhuman. Their predatory
qualities, described above, come with related features that can be seen as
weaknesses. They are often hyper-sensitive to insults, and react violently
to them. They are impulsive, and often do not consider the consequences
of their actions. They like excitement, and enjoy doing risky things. They
often do not have clear plans for achieving their grandiose goals.

Such features may help to explain why some fraudsters pursue schemes
that are doomed to failure. Ponzi schemes, for example, can develop naturally from a legitimate business as the result of a few impulsive decisions, like
making risky investments that lose money, and then covering up the losses
and paying old investors with new investors' money – once the fraudster has
done this a few times, he is virtually trapped into a cycle of maintaining the
fraud to avoid discovery, without any idea of how he is going to get out of
it. A psychopath, it is thought, would feel more comfortable in such a trap
than a 'normal' fraudster because of his lack of fear, an enjoyment of the
risks, and a lack of thought about the likely eventual consequences.

Unfortunately, unless a fraudster is properly tested and the results published, we cannot say for sure if a given individual, such as Bernie Madoff,
is actually a psychopath. The word gets bandied about too freely in the
popular media, and Madoff has even discussed the question with an interviewer, claiming that a psychiatrist had told him, 'You are absolutely not a
sociopath' (the term 'sociopath' is often used to refer to non-violent psychopaths). It would be typical of a psychopath to tell such a story, but this
doesn't help us; it really isn't constructive for a non-expert to attempt a
diagnosis. The best that can be said is there is a *prima facie* case for Madoff
possibly being a psychopath, given his charm, deceitfulness, recklessness
and the doubtful sincerity of the remorse he has expressed.

Investors, especially the kind of investor who assumes that finance professionals will always act rationally, should get to know something about
psychopathy, because it refers to a type of person who not only would make
a very convincing fraudster but is also capable of committing fraud in circumstances that a 'normal' fraudster would find too risky or too stressful. Many
of the frauds discussed in this book were likely to be discovered eventually,

so a 'rational' fraudster who wanted to avoid this would look elsewhere; the fact that the frauds were committed anyway should alert us to the fact that it is possible, perhaps even probable, fraudsters often ignore such calculations; some in this latter group may in fact be psychopaths.

Routine activity theory

Despairing of the possibility of penetrating the psychology of fraudsters, many researchers have turned to different kinds of analysis, such as examining the situations in which fraud occur. One such approach is routine activity theory, proposed by Cohen and Felson in the late 1970s. The theory assumes that perpetrators will act rationally, assess all the risks carefully, and only commit a crime if the benefits of doing so outweigh the risks and/or costs of getting caught. As mentioned above, it is clear that not all fraudsters do behave rationally in this way, but nevertheless it may be a large number of fraudsters do make such assessments. The theory proposes that there are three factors involved in crime:

1 the opportunity to commit a crime
2 the absence of effective guards
3 the motive to commit a crime.

According to Cohen and Felson, crime rates don't go down in times of prosperity simply because there are more opportunities to commit crime. These opportunities become more apparent during routine, recurring activities, such as working in an office each day, when victims and victimisers are brought together repeatedly. If there are no strong guardians to protect the victims, the criminals will commit a crime. Thus, the theory attempts to predict the situations where crimes are likely to cluster.

In 1995, Nick Leeson, a futures trader based in Singapore, brought down his employer, the venerable merchant bank, Barings. Leeson had made a series of unauthorised and risky trades on behalf of the bank, apparently in pursuit of an increased bonus that would be forthcoming if he achieved increased trading profits. When he started to make losses, he disguised them and then tried to trade his way out of trouble, which created further losses and resulted in Baring's' collapse owing £827 million, twice the available trading capital of the bank. An analysis using routine activity theory would emphasise the absence of an effective system of control and supervision within Barings; it is alleged that senior executives did not appreciate the potential size of the liabilities created by derivatives trading, and the internal controls should have spotted Leeson's activities before they got out of hand. The theory suggests analysing job roles may reveal weaknesses in the control system that indicate a conjunction between an opportunity for wrongdoing and the absence of adequate controls; and indeed, Leeson had sufficient autonomy in the Singapore office to be able to disguise his reckless trading from his superiors.

Routine activity theory has focused attention on the 'guardian' factor, with the rationale that there are likely to be more crimes in situations where there are weak guardians. This has some relevance to the investment world, because it is very striking that there are fashions in investment fraud, with one specific fraud type being in vogue for a few years before it gives way to another. This variation in the type of fraud may be linked to the waxing and waning of governance in specific areas. For example, the sub-prime mortgage crisis of 2007 was in large part due to a gradual, but drastic, relaxation of the regulation of the mortgage lending industry in the US. This reduced regulation allowed intermediaries to commit a range of frauds on a large scale that would never have been permitted under earlier regulatory regimes. Thus someone with intimate knowledge of the state of the industry's regulation might have been able to foresee that there would be an increase in fraud.

This doesn't help us much as individual investors, because we generally don't have an intimate knowledge of all the regulatory authorities that are supposed to protect our investments! Perhaps we should. We certainly need to be aware of the basic protections, such as the details of compensation schemes for bank deposits. It may seem obvious, but it is important to appreciate that regulators and investor protection schemes in different countries work differently from one another. Deposit protection in Ruritania, say, will not be identical to deposit protection in the UK, and may well not be covered by UK schemes. The Icesave customers in the UK who lost money in 2008 received compensation from the UK government, but it was not obliged to give this money under any scheme; it stepped in when it emerged that the Icelandic government was not at that time willing to offer compensation to foreign savers. These little details really matter when you are deciding where to invest – some investor protection schemes are not worth the paper they are written on.

Nigerian scams – a different type of fraudster altogether?

Although the notorious Nigerian fraud gangs have not penetrated very deeply into the regular investment world, their creativity and talent for financial fraud suggests that they may eventually arrive there. In the meantime, it is worthwhile considering the unusual methods and structures of these gangs to see whether or not they offer any insight into fraudster psychology.

Since the 1980s Nigerian gangs have been operating internationally, duping victims across the world into handing over larger and larger sums of money. Although the UK has been a major target for these scams because of its historical connections with Nigeria, the gangs have penetrated very widely indeed; I once spent a week in Penang, Malaysia, watching a Nigerian group who had just been expelled from Thailand continue their activities from a local internet café.

The scams these gangs operate are diverse and often innovative; the main one is advance fee fraud, also known as the Spanish prisoner scam. This scam existed long before the Nigerians lighted upon it. In its traditional form, the victim is told that the fraudster needs to ransom or rescue a wealthy relative who is being held in Spain; if the victim will put up the money to secure the release of the relative, he will receive a huge reward. The classic Nigerian versions, known as '419 frauds' because they fall under section 419 of Nigeria's penal code, generally involve approaching a foreigner, often by email, to ask for help in a venture. Typically this will involve an elaborate story about a huge sum of money that is blocked or frozen; if the victim can stump up a few thousand to help free the money, he or she will receive millions in commission. Some victims are tricked into paying multiple sums over to the fraudsters on various pretexts before they realise it is a scam; some victims never do realise that they have been cheated. The stories told by the fraudsters range from the ridiculous (a share in Saddam Hussein's private wealth) to the plausible (intercepting calls to Nigeria and telling the caller that the person they are calling has been in a traffic accident and needs money urgently). Emails and letters are sent out on a massive scale, and even the most unbelievable story seems to find a few takers. According to the FBI, 419 scams have netted more than a billion dollars in the US in total, while a Dutch firm estimates that the UK lost $520 million to the scammers in 2005 alone. Although the Nigerian authorities are attempting to crack down on these scams, Western governments have been less responsive. This is partly because much of the fraud is believed to go unreported, and also because there seems to be a general feeling that anyone greedy or foolish enough to fall for such a scheme deserves what they get. Often the emails and letters are full of obviously false statements and ridiculous mistakes. Frequently they invite the victim to participate in a crime, such as illegally diverting public funds from an African government. The victims get plenty of warning, in other words, that the fraudsters may not be who they say they are. Nigerians sometimes claim that victims are deceived because they are racist and assume that the fraudsters are asking for their help out of a child-like African naivety. This may be true in some cases, but in others it seems more likely that the victims themselves were simply very gullible.

Dismissing Nigerian fraud because it seems to prey only on the extremely gullible is a mistake. Beneath the surface, the gangs are becoming increasingly adventurous and sophisticated. For example, they are known to be active in 'phishing', trying to obtain account details and PINs from victims over the internet by, for example, sending them an email that appears to have come from their bank. They are also very active in international credit card fraud, often taking care only to make relatively small purchases, say under £1,000, to avoid attention from the authorities.

The gangs are said to be loosely structured and 'flat', without a rigid hierarchy. Groups may coalesce under one leader to carry out a particular scam, and then dissolve into other groups in which other members take the leadership role. Some informants claim, however, that there are 'gangmasters' who seek out computer-literate English-speaking youngsters to work as 'foot soldiers' for years before being allowed to conduct their own scams. Nigeria itself suffers from rampant endemic corruption and it is often difficult to tell where crime ends and the formal economy begins. Many policemen and office functionaries take bribes as a matter of course. In what has become a disastrously dysfunctional society, many people feel justified in participating in scams in order to survive. Corruption in the country also helps to make it a safe haven from which to operate, or to which to return with ill-gotten gains. Parcels sent via carriers from Nigeria to the UK are said to consist largely of forged documents, which are then used by other gang members for their various scams. This gives an indication of the industrial scale of the fraud: every day, thousands of documents, including identity documents, phoney cheques, and official letters, are produced for a huge number of ongoing scams. Much of the material going the other way, from the UK to Nigeria, consists of items purchased fraudulently, according to customs officials. The division of labour is well organised, with different people, often in different countries, specialising in particular tasks, such as writing letters, forging official documents, arranging travel, and holding meetings. Victims are often encouraged to visit Nigeria, where they are then vulnerable to all kinds of extortion even if they are unwilling to close the deal they are being offered.

Scamming in Nigeria, which has a population of 162 million, is so widespread that it is perhaps more helpful to view it as a social phenomenon than to attempt to analyse the fraudsters' personalities. Reports suggest that common attitudes among the scammers include the views that they are not to blame for the victims' greed, the victims are the descendants of exploitative imperialists, or the scam is payback for the slave trade. In other words, the victims deserve to be cheated. Such attitudes are common enough in the developing world; what makes the Nigerian scammers interesting is that they are adapting, very rapidly and very creatively, to the globalisation of world finance. They are resourceful, smart, and well-travelled. They have global networks, and they keep the money moving – it is claimed that proceeds from smaller scams (many 419 frauds are thought to net only a few thousand pounds a time) into bigger ventures, such as heroin smuggling, in which Nigerians have become very active. They are willing to try new scams, and some clearly have aspirations to get into the higher end of financial services. It would not be surprising if they succeed – watch out for Nigerian scammers at the riskier end of investment – such as commodities, financial derivatives and spread betting – in the years to come.

The problem with plausibility

Law enforcers use profiling with some success to identify types of individuals who are likely to commit specific crimes. The trouble with this approach, from the investor's point of view, is that we don't often have the opportunity to really assess the personalities of the people who handle our investments. Warren Buffett, the famous investor, emphasises the importance of good character in the executives who run the companies in which he invests, but, as one of the richest men in the world, he has unusually good access to these people.

Most of us have to make do with much more indirect evidence, such as the plausibility and internal consistency of the investment offers. What many of us fail to do, however, is to verify the facts. Plausibility is an important factor – who would want to invest in an implausible scheme? – but, as we have seen, there are personality types who are extremely skilled at creating spurious plausibility.

A charming, clever, witty, confidence-inspiring financial star may be genuine, but he or she may in fact be a psychopath recklessly exploiting investors in a scheme that is bound to end badly. Routine activity theory has highlighted the rather obvious, but nevertheless very important, point that there is likely to be more fraud in situations where controls and supervision are inadequate. A good rule of thumb for investors is that controls are likely to be more relaxed during bull markets: it is when things are going really well and everybody seems to be making money and it becomes a racing certainty there will be more fraud. And we should not forget

> A charming, clever, witty, confidence-inspiring financial star may be genuine, but he or she may in fact be a psychopath recklessly exploiting investors in a scheme that is bound to end badly.

that during bull markets the intermediaries tend to relax their standards, too. For example, during the dotcom bubble of the late 1990s I spent a day in Hong Kong with a stock analyst at a major US investment bank who painted an absurdly optimistic picture of how successful a number of dotcom companies were going to be. Within months, some of his favourites had collapsed. The analyst's arguments were based on glowing estimates of future growth that a child could see through, but he showed no sign of embarrassment – he evidently thought that his ridiculous stories would be believed. Does this mean that he was some kind of fraudster? Probably not. It is more likely as a stock analyst on the 'sell side' (the departments in financial institutions that sell investment products and advice to the public) he was simply expected, as part of company policy, to talk up these stocks. So was the investment bank committing fraud? Not exactly – it is not necessarily fraudulent to make optimistic stock recommendations, although when the dotcom bubble finally popped a number of analysts were in fact found to have acted improperly. When everyone else thinks that a certain industry can only go up, it just isn't very good business for an institution to be gloomy and suspicious – that's the investor's job! But we should not make the mistake of thinking that such advice is always impartial, or institutions see it as their duty to blow the whistle on possible crooks. As we have seen (Chapter 3), a number of institutions conducted a careful analysis of Madoff's investment business and concluded that something was wrong. They chose to avoid Madoff, but did not denounce him.

Globalisation and the internet have given millions of people in developing countries access to the West. In the financial world this is seen as good for business, but globalisation brings new risks with it. We may be at the beginning of a new era of frauds emanating from developing countries. In addition to the Nigerian fraudsters discussed above, there has been a striking increase in telephone fraud coming from the call centre cities in India, such as Bangalore. Westerners are telephoned at home from a person claiming to work for a famous software company. The victim is told that there is a virus problem and is persuaded to switch on their computer and then follow instructions given by the caller. This results in the download of software to 'fix' the non-existent virus, and then a demand for money. It would not take an enormous effort of the imagination for a well-connected financial fraudster to devise a scam that exploited this valuable Indian resource: a low-cost sales force of internet-savvy English speakers well out of reach of the authorities in the target countries. Watch this space!

5

Yielding to temptation: the Allen Stanford story

Yes, I have to say it's fun being a billionaire …
R. Allen Stanford, CEO Stanford Financial Group

Offshore jurisdictions

Periodically, politicians in the UK start to make public announcements about the wickedness of businesspeople who use offshore jurisdictions as a method of legal tax avoidance. This is largely disingenuous. Not all offshore jurisdictions are acutely vulnerable to corruption: Jersey, Singapore and Bermuda, for example, have high standards and are well run. Legitimate offshore business is huge; some 8% of all wealth under management is thought to be held offshore, an estimated $7 trillion. Some 700,000 companies are registered in the British Virgin Islands. Many thousands of hedge funds are registered in the Cayman Islands. Almost all the world's major banks and corporations have offshore operations. It is ridiculous to pretend, as some onshore politicians do to their domestic audiences, that the offshore financial world is a marginalised, criminal arena that has nothing to do with regular business; in fact, the offshore world is an integral part of international business and finance.

Nevertheless, offshore finance does have a shady side. Figures associated with many political parties are known to avail themselves of offshore facilities. As one retired offshore tax lawyer once commented to me, 'offshore jurisdictions will be allowed to continue to exist as long as politicians and businesspeople continue to need somewhere offshore to park their funds.' But offshore jurisdictions are not merely places to park money. So long as the world consists of nation states that compete economically and have conflicting regulatory systems, there will be many legitimate reasons to practise 'regulations arbitrage' by locating some operations in a lightly regulated offshore jurisdiction, just as the world's shipping industry could not function without the existence of 'flags of convenience' – flags of convenience are offered by countries such as Panama and Liberia that allow foreign merchant ships to register with them, generally reducing labour costs and regulatory burdens. Nevertheless, both flags of convenience and offshore finance provide scope for criminal and fraudulent activity, and if we are now entering an era of economic protectionism and high regulation, in contrast to the trend of deregulation and globalisation during the last three decades, then such wrongdoing could actually increase along with an increase in the legitimate use of such jurisdictions, as people seek to avoid high regulations in 'onshore' countries.

> 'Offshore jurisdictions will be allowed to continue to exist as long as politicians and businesspeople continue to need somewhere offshore to park their funds.'

Many of the frauds discussed in this book involved the use of offshore jurisdictions, from Bernie Madoff's European connections, to Dennis Levine's use of offshore bank accounts for insider trading, to Crazy Eddie's transfer of his secret profits abroad. In this chapter Allen Stanford's operations in the Caribbean, which are a particularly egregious example of how offshore jurisdictions can be exploited by a fraudster, will be examined in detail. First, it is important to note the essential problem in dealing with frauds that have an international dimension: it is often very difficult for any country's regulator to obtain information about the fraudster from a foreign jurisdiction, in particular from an offshore jurisdiction that has high secrecy laws, or to pursue a fraudster abroad. In practice, most regulatory bodies do not have the clout to pursue such problems, but the SEC and other US agencies have a long record of pressurising foreign authorities, with some degree of success (in the 1980s the SEC, for example, was able to persuade Bank Leu in the Bahamas to divulge that Dennis Levine was the account holder of accounts used for insider trading – see Chapter 2). As we will see in the Allen Stanford story, however, applying pressure and pursuing litigation in other countries is slow, enabling the fraudster to take evasive action.

Good old boys

In Europe we tend to raise our eyebrows at a 'new' bank. If it wasn't around during the Napoleonic Wars, we tend to feel, then, that it can't really be quite right. But much of this sense of tradition is illusory. Over the last few decades the extraordinary relaxation of financial regulation across the world has engendered a maelstrom of buy-outs, mergers and entries into new financial areas, to the extent that very few banks remain which are as stuffy and cautious as they used to be. In the Americas, on the other hand, newness is not necessarily seen as a bad thing. The fact that Allen Stanford and his senior team projected themselves as good old boys from the deep South, God-fearing Southern Baptists who believed hard work and honesty could take them to the top in the world of financial services, was appealing to the group's main customer base in the US and Latin America.

The 'Forbes 400 Richest People in America' 2008 feature on Stanford presents a classic rags-to-riches story. 'The muscular, 6-foot-4 Stanford, whose eyes bulge when he's excited' was born in Mexia, a backwater in East Texas, made his first money at the age of 13 chopping wood, and then gave it all to a family whose house had burned down. He had studied finance at Baylor University, Texas, where he met his Chief Financial Officer, James D. Davis, and later, after failing in a health club venture, he joined the family business, a small property and insurance concern. The big break allegedly came in the early 1980s when Stanford and his father bought up as much property as they could during a property market crash in Houston and then made several hundred million dollars selling it off over the next decade as prices recovered, according to the Forbes article.

And that's when our story really begins. Stanford used the profits he had allegedly made to set up a wealth management business, attracting customers in Mexico, Venezuela and Ecuador as well as back home in the US. 'Stanford's investment strategy can be described as sure and steady', the Forbes piece assures us, 'it sets an internal return on investment targets based on the market environment ... uses leverage sparingly, and holdings are diversified across countries and currencies.' After the dotcom collapse in 2000, Stanford managed to achieve returns of 10% or more annually, we are told. Stanford complains that as a 'maverick, rich Texan in the Caribbean' he is an easy target for censure, and he then proceeds to bat away various criticisms, such as the allegation he had falsely claimed to be related to the founder of Stanford University, and his long-running feud with Antigua's prime minister. It is pointed out that Stanford received a knighthood from Antigua in 2006. The big excitement in 2008, however, was Stanford's plan to inject big money into the world of cricket, which offered great potential as 'an international branding tool for his company'.

In 2008, then, Allen Stanford could be seen as a fairly familiar type of tycoon; slightly megalomaniacal, perhaps, but not worryingly so. In fact, since he had avoided the chaos and scandal of the sub-prime crash in 2007, he could be regarded as a welcome change from all those oily investment bankers on Wall Street who seemed to be – and, indeed, were – so deeply mired in allegations of dirty politics and financial corruption at that time. Investment salesman Charles Hazlett's concerns about the firm had been aired in an arbitration case a few years earlier, but this had not been widely publicised, and in early 2008 two of the firm's financial advisers, D. Mark Tidwell and Charles W. Rawl, were alleging in a court case that the Stanford group was involved in unethical practices. Indeed, there had also been a number of other cases making similar allegations brought to the US Financial Industry Regulatory Authority (FINRA) by unhappy ex-employees, but average investors might not have learned of these or, if they had, could easily dismiss them as typical of the industry – after all, big financial services firms are always getting sued by disgruntled ex-employees.

But what of the Certificates of Deposit (CDs) that the group promoted so industriously? Why would any ordinary investor put a large sum of money into CDs offered by an offshore bank? There seem to be a number of answers. First, although CDs are not well known in Europe, in the US they are a popular method of saving; you purchase a CD from a conventional bank for a fixed period of time, and receive a fixed rate of interest. In most cases your investment is insured by the US Securities Investor Protection Corporation (SIPC) or the Federal Deposit Insurance Corporation (FDIC). CDs, therefore, are widely perceived as a safe, boring instrument in which to put your money, earning a low rate of interest. Although Stanford's CDs appear not to have been insured by SIPC or FDIC, they had a very attractive feature: you could cash out at any time without penalties. Furthermore, the interest rate offered was substantially higher than the going rate back in the US – a warning sign to some, but an attractive inducement to others. Many investors also believed, according to the Receiver, that the money they handed over in return for the CD would be held in some kind of individual account. This is not, in fact, how CDs work. CDs are in essence debts owed by a bank to investors, and are not associated with a segregated account in the name of an investor.

According to the testimony of Stan Kauffman, a customer of Stanford's, Stanford representatives reassured him about the company's offshore status by stating that the deposits were insured by Lloyd's of London and the group was heavily regulated in the many jurisdictions in which it was active. Although the bank was in Antigua, the Stanford Financial Group was based in Houston, Texas. The sales literature Kauffman was given had been approved by the US regulator FINRA, and the sales representatives were registered with the US regulator the SEC, and had an obligation to recommend the most suitable investments for the needs of individual customers. According to Kauffman, the facts that part of the group was managed in the US, many of the senior managers were US citizens, and the Advisory Board included many respectable figures, such as a former assistant Secretary of State, also helped to convince him everything was above-board and properly regulated.

For 'mom and pop' investors in the US, often approaching retirement, Stanford's CDs could be seen as a safe, conservative investment offering a welcome higher return. It appears that not all of Stanford's depositors were middle-aged, middle-class Americans. As we have seen, from the beginning Stanford had targeted Latin American clients as well. Latin American investors often suffer from serious problems in their own countries, in particular from volatile currencies, arbitrary taxation and a changeable political climate. For many Latin American investors, the solution is to get some of their wealth abroad, and offshore banks in the Caribbean seem to be an ideal solution. For example, Venezuela under Hugo Chavez has experienced a series of measures designed to deprive wealthy Venezeluans of their assets, and this group had to get as much of its money out of the country as it could.

> For 'mom and pop' investors in the US, often approaching retirement, Stanford's CDs could be seen as a safe, conservative investment offering a welcome higher return.

Other customer segments that are naturally drawn to offshore jurisdictions include individuals trying to protect their assets in a divorce, tax avoiders, tax evaders, and, notoriously in the Caribbean, drug traffickers and money launderers. However, this kind of activity goes with the territory in many tax havens, and no substantial evidence has appeared to suggest that Stanford knowingly provided banking services to drug lords or other criminals.

What is clear, though, is that Stanford customers received red carpet treatment. Arriving at the offices, investors were sent to a parking spot bearing their own name, and then whisked through acres of marble and mahogany grandeur to a special cinema to watch a film about the firm's high moral integrity, inherited from Allen Stanford's grandfather who had founded an insurance company in the 1930s. After this, you were treated to a luxurious meal in the private dining room. Larger investors might be flown to Antigua in one of the group's jets to visit the bank, staying at the glorious Jumby Bay island resort, and meeting the great man himself, the picture of confidence and integrity.

Back in the 1980s, flushed with the success of his Texas property deals, Allen Stanford had set up the Guardian International Bank on the Caribbean island of Montserrat as part of his wealth management business. He made his old college room-mate, James M. Davis, the Controller of the bank. Soon afterwards, according to Davis, Stanford asked him to make false entries in the general ledger with the aim of giving the regulators a false impression of the bank's income and investments. The business of the Guardian bank was essentially the same as the later incarnations of the group: to sell CDs to investors who paid a higher-than-normal interest rate. Allen Stanford had begun to siphon some of the depositors' money out of the bank to fund a number of his own property deals, apparently with the intention of repaying the money when the property deals came good.

In 1990 a British regulatory crackdown on offshore banking in Montserrat (the island is still a British Overseas Territory) prompted Stanford to move the bank to Antigua, where it was renamed the Stanford International Bank. The Montserrat government had told Stanford that it was about to revoke the Guardian International Bank's licence; Stanford acted quickly, moving the bank to Antigua, surrendering the Montserrat banking licence before it was taken from him, and claiming publicly the move was due to the devastation caused by Hurricane Hugo.

Late in the same year, Davis found that the bank's true assets were less than half of those reported; Stanford was set on investing depositors' money in a wide range of businesses, mostly owned by himself, mostly located in the Caribbean, and mostly losing money. To keep these schemes going, Stanford needed the bank's CD business to grow. He took a hands-on approach to marketing, reviewing sales spreadsheets daily with managers, and instituting elaborate reward schemes for successful salespeople. In the early 1990s Stanford produced a forged insurance policy to assure sales staff and clients that the bank's assets were insured (they weren't), and on one occasion ordered James Davis to fly to London to fax a phoney confirmation to a potential depositor the insurance underwriter actually existed (it didn't). Stanford personally adjusted the group's financial statements on occasion to give a false picture, as well as pressing Davis and other accountants to do so.

In 1995 Stanford opened the Stanford Group Company in the US to sell the CDs to American customers; the two main bases for this firm were Houston and Miami, but there was also a large number of smaller offices, mainly in the south of the country. As the business grew, the arrangements to conceal what was happening to the money became increasingly elaborate. Davis, who was to start his own church, met a young woman, Laura Pendergest (now Pendergest-Holt) at a Baptist church meeting in Baldwyn Mississippi, and eventually recruited her. As Chief Investment Officer, Pendergest supervised a team of analysts (actually her and Davis's relatives and fellow church members, who had little financial experience) based in Mississippi, and, purportedly, managed the bank's entire portfolio. In fact, Pendergest's team only managed a small fraction of the bank's investments (an estimated 15%), and were expressly instructed not to reveal this information to anyone, not even financial advisers working for the firm. Individuals within the organisation who gained an inkling of what was really going on were warned to stop asking awkward questions or face the sack. There was a sustained effort by a small core of insiders – Allen Stanford, James Davis and a few others – to create the impression to customers, employees and regulators that the bank's investment funds were being prudently and professionally managed by the Mississippi team, when in fact the bulk of the money was going into Allen Stanford's own private schemes.

One might suppose that customers and employees were relatively easy to deceive; customers rely on the regulatory apparatus to protect them from fraudsters, and employees, including the well-paid 'financial advisers' (actually CD salespeople), had a strong disincentive to ask too many questions. As we have seen (page 9), when Charles Hazlett, an experienced investment salesman for Stanford, began to sense that investors' legitimate questions were not being answered satisfactorily, it was not long before he had to leave the firm. But what about the external accountants and the government regulators in the US and Antigua? These people are professionally trained to spot wrongdoing; couldn't they have spotted problems early on?

Perhaps they did; but Allen Stanford had some rather interesting solutions for coping with them, too. Possibly as a result of his experience of the unwelcome attentions of the British regulators in Montserrat, when Stanford relocated the bank to Antigua in 1990 he seems to have been determined from the start to ensure that none of the locals would cause him any problems. Even before the move to Antigua, the bank's external auditor was Charlesworth Hewlett, who ran a small accounting firm in Antigua. According to the prosecution, the Montserrat regulators repeatedly asked Stanford to use a larger auditing firm but he refused to do so because Hewlett was willing to give the bank's phoney accounts a clean bill of health in return for large fees – allegedly a total of $3.4 million was paid to Hewlett, who died in 2009.

Stanford embarked upon a charm offensive to persuade the island's government to let him operate freely. He purchased the Bank of Antigua, a failing local bank serving the islanders, for $50 million, and lent the government $40 million which he later agreed to write off. Soon, he received his banking licence and residency permit. Antigua, a tiny island paradise, relies largely on tourism to survive, but locals are relatively poor: GDP per capita in 1998 was only $8,500. Allen Stanford spent money liberally on the island, endearing himself to rich and poor alike, buying large tracts of land, setting up restaurants and a cricket stadium, helping to build a hospital, paying $48,000 for Prime Minister Lester Bird's US medical expenses, making substantial interest-free loans and political contributions to at least ten other senior government officials and later buying the island's newspaper, the *Antigua Sun*.

During the 1990s Antigua was trying to diversify into offshore banking, and when it ran into trouble with outfits allegedly linked to the Russian mafia, Allen Stanford stepped in, helping to write new offshore trust laws and becoming, in 1997, the Chairman of the government's Antiguan Offshore Financial Sector Planning Committee. As Chairman, Stanford appointed a task force to clean up Antiguan banking, and every member of the task force was a close associate of Stanford (there were no locals on the task force). A new regulatory body, the International Financial Sector Authority (IFSA), was set up, and in a stroke worthy of the seventeenth-century pirate Henry Morgan, Stanford managed to have himself made Chairman of this organisation as well. The IFSA proved remarkably resistant to Stanford at first. Althea Crick, the island's locally born chief banking regulator until 2002, persistently refused to accept bribes and perks, such as upgrades to first class on flights to London. When Stanford ordered the seizure of his banking competitors' records through the IFSA, Crick refused to allow him to copy them, and he had to send men to break into the IFSA offices at night and take the records away. On another occasion, according to Crick, when she told Allen Stanford to his face that she would not be influenced by him, 'he held my hand, and looked me straight in the eye and said, "You remind me so much of myself."' After Crick resigned in 2002 and a new regulator, the Financial Services Regulatory Commission (FSRC), had been set up to replace the IFSA, Stanford managed again to get some of his own ex-employees into key positions in the organisation, and developed a close relationship with the man who became the FSRC's head in 2003, locally born Leroy King, a former ambassador to the US who had also been a Bank America executive in New York. According to James Davis, during 2003 Stanford and King participated in a curious voodoo-type ceremony in which they became blood brothers, ensuring that King, and another FSRC official who was present, would help protect Stanford's businesses from the prying eyes of regulators both in Antigua and abroad in return for bribes. Leroy King was to prove a loyal associate over the years, providing a stream of information to Stanford about the FSRC's dealing with foreign regulators, and helping to confuse and deflect regulatory investigations into Stanford's activities. For example, when, in 2005, the SEC, the US stock market regulator, made a number of requests to the FSRC for information about the Stanford group, Leroy King immediately warned Stanford and was provided by Stanford's people with a draft FSRC reply to the SEC. In 2006 Stanford transferred part of his business to St Croix in the Virgin Islands, and began to spend less time in Antigua.

The 'noughties' had been an extraordinary period of growth for the Stanford group, as the sales drive gathered speed; by the end of 2008, it had sold CDs worth a total of more than $7.2 billion. In 2008 the global financial crisis really began to bite. The major stock markets declined rapidly, and although Stanford claimed that the bank's investments were immune to any downturn, CD sales slowed and the number of customers redeeming their CDs increased alarmingly. During the year, some $2 billion had to be paid back to customers. By October 2008, Stanford had serious liquidity problems; the bank was running out of money to pay back customers, and Stanford's private businesses could not be sold. Together they were losing over $1 million a day. From a business point of view, this is a familiar problem: in a financial downturn everything tends to go wrong at once, with asset values, income and liquidity evaporating simultaneously, and powerful business associates beginning to turn against you. Frans Vingerhoedt, President of Stanford Caribbean Investments LLC, the man who is alleged to have first introduced Stanford to the idea of starting an offshore bank in the Caribbean in the 1980s, sent an email to Stanford in early 2009 warning of the need to give preference to 'certain people in certain countries' – presumably powerful people in Latin America – because 'there are real bullets out there with my name on'.

Stanford fought hard to save his empire. Towards the end of 2008 he announced that he was injecting $741 million of his own money into the bank. This was based on a deal in which the bank had purchased, for $63.5 million in June, some raw land in Antigua that Stanford wished to develop as a resort. The plan was that the bank would transfer the land to Stanford personally, who would then sell the land back to the bank through a series of companies at the much larger price of $3.2 billion, thereby wiping out the $2 billion he owed the bank and providing the capital injection. During the court cases the US government has presented this deal as an out-and-out sham, which Stanford appears to deny. The land in question, which had been purchased from Malaysian wheeler-dealer Tan Kay Hock, was the beautiful island of Guiana (five miles square), which Stanford had been lobbying for years to develop into an upmarket resort. As Nigel Hamilton-Smith, one of the bank's receivers in Antigua, commented later, the increased value depended on obtaining final permission to develop – 'it could be US$50 million, US$250 million, US$1 billion. I just don't know' – and thus it appears that Allen Stanford may genuinely have been about to pull off a value-adding master stroke to fend off the bank's collapse. He continued to live large, allegedly spending $250,000 on a Christmas holiday with his extended family, dropping $515,000 on gambling and jewellery during a manic week in Las Vegas in January 2009 and then flying to Libya in an attempt to obtain funding for the bank from Colonel Gaddafi.

Were Stanford's continual protestations of innocence merely part of his legal defence or the result of delusional thinking, or was the SEC's accusation that he was running a Ponzi scheme an oversimplification designed, perhaps, to appeal to a financially illiterate jury? It seems clear that Allen Stanford consistently deceived his customers about how their money was being invested, and it was established in court that the firms had broken numerous financial regulations in the US and elsewhere, and Stanford and his close associates knowingly published false information about the bank's performance. However, as the SEC's own definition asserts, 'a Ponzi scheme is an investment fraud that involves the payment of purported returns to existing investors from funds contributed by new investors … In many Ponzi schemes, the fraudsters focus on attracting new money to make promised payments to earlier-stage investors and to use for personal expenses, instead of engaging in any legitimate investment activity.' Stanford, and his lawyer, Ali Fazel, have maintained that he did indeed engage in legitimate investment activity: through his network of companies he set up a number of banks in Latin America, for example in Peru, Venezuela, Ecuador and Panama, and also, although largely in secret, he had funnelled large sums of money that had been received from CD purchasers into real estate deals, especially in the Caribbean, that he personally controlled. If these deals had come right, perhaps Stanford would have been able to pay back the vast loans (estimated to be just under $2 billion) that the bank had made to him personally. If he genuinely believed this was going to occur, then one can have some sympathy with Allen Stanford's passionate declarations that he was not running a Ponzi scheme. This is little comfort to purchasers of Stanford CDs, and does not exonerate Stanford from his clear deception of his customers, but on this reading it is easier to understand how he could have had such confidence in the long-term future of the operation: the Stanford group of companies was going to continue to go from strength to strength, and the Caribbean property deals were going to produce a bonanza in profits beyond the dreams of avarice. In some respects many big time property tycoons operate in this way, especially in tropical paradises – if you can get some influence with a government, you may be able fix it so that you become the main beneficiary of major development projects. In this light, Stanford's assertion that he was 'more of a developer at heart than a banker' rings true, and his behaviour might be seen more as the risk-taking, rule-breaking behaviour of a narcissistic entrepreneur rather than as a deliberate attempt to commit fraud. Stanford may indeed be justified in claiming that the agencies involved in prosecuting him and attempting to wind up his companies have damaged the value of the schemes in which he invested.

Making sense of Stanford

As the Stanford story illustrates, having officials in your pocket in offshore jurisdictions will not protect you forever, especially if you still need to do business with 'onshore' customers. However, the fact that Stanford's bank was based offshore appears to have been a major factor in repeated decisions by the SEC not to act against him during an eight-year period. In 1997, 1998, 2002 and 2004, investigators at the SEC's district office at Fort Worth, Texas conducted four separate examinations of Stanford's activities and decided each time that the CDs were probably a Ponzi scheme. Each time, the examination group at Fort Worth asked the enforcement division to open a formal investigation of Stanford's companies but were turned down (except in 1998, when an investigation came to life briefly, only to be closed down after three months). An SEC inquiry into this failure found that senior managers at Fort Worth had discouraged pursuing Stanford because they were under pressure from head office to increase the number of successful prosecutions, and they believed the Stanford case would be very difficult to pursue. Thus, the fact that Stanford's bank was based offshore, making it a challenge to obtain documents, was given as a reason for not investigating.

Significantly, the report found that Spencer Barasch, head of enforcement at Fort Worth between 1998 and 2005, 'had played a significant role in multiple decisions over the years to quash investigations of Stanford', and had then tried several times to act as Stanford's legal representative after he left the SEC. Barasch did act for Stanford in 2006 briefly until he was warned by the SEC that this was unethical. In connection with this, Barasch was fined by the SEC in 2012 and banned for a year from appearing and practising as a lawyer before it. This kind of behaviour is perhaps symptomatic of the atmosphere and institutional culture at the SEC in recent years. According to the Project on Government Oversight, a government watchdog, 219 former SEC officials have left the organisation since 2006 to help clients that are being examined or investigated by the SEC.

Even on the most charitable interpretation, this phenomenon cannot be welcome to investors who look to the SEC for protection. It is even more disturbing that some investigators at the SEC had spotted the big clue with Stanford – returns and commissions on his CDs were much too high for them to be safe investments – repeatedly over many years without being able to persuade their bosses to do much about it. The SEC only began a proper investigation in 2005, under Barasch's successor, and even then it did not occur to anyone to perform due diligence on Stanford's investments, which would probably have revealed sufficient problems to enable the SEC to ban Stanford Group Company (the onshore sales organisation) from handling sales of CDs issued by Stanford's bank in Antigua.

> Even on the most charitable interpretation, this phenomenon cannot be welcome to investors who look to the SEC for protection.

In the final analysis, then, it was not so much the fact that Stanford operated offshore that kept him from being shut down for many years, as the inability of a provincial office of the SEC to prosecute any but the 'quick hit' cases. This is a staggering, outrageous institutional failure of the world's most powerful financial regulator; when it is considered along with many other failures, not least the SEC's long inaction over Madoff (see

Chapter 3), it is plain that the SEC is in great need of reform. Until this happens, investors can have little confidence that the SEC can guard them against large-scale fraud.

6

Shamanagement: financial wizardry to create paper profits

Innocent people never have fears when they go to face injustice.

Asil Nadir, former CEO of Polly Peck, when returning to the UK in 2010 to face trial

To a certain kind of mind, raising money from the public by issuing shares looks like a remarkably easy way to get rich quick. The truth is that most of the time it is a massively expensive exercise, which places a very heavy burden of responsibility on a company's executives, and rightly so. In boom times, however, raising money in the market becomes much easier. With so much money seeking investments that offer high returns, standards drop and investors become less choosy. Hot money sloshes about looking for a home without taking the proper precautions of 'due diligence', and a lot of it ends up under the control of unsavoury characters.

If you already control a company with a soaring share price, there's an even more attractive route to financial stardom: mergers and acquisitions. During boom times many firms attempt to grow rapidly by buying other companies as quickly as possible. They are able to obtain the funds for the purchases because of the inflated market valuation of their own companies.

> And a remarkably large number of acquisitive firms have eventually collapsed amid accusations of fraud.

While some mergers and acquisitions (M&A) have proved to be sound long-term moves, many have not, unravelling during the next stock market slump. And a remarkably large number of acquisitive firms have eventually collapsed amid accusations of fraud.

In this chapter we will look at two major cases, both of which have been in the news but have roots going back many years: Olympus and Polly Peck.

The Olympus scandal

Late in 2011 Michael Woodford, a long-time employee, became the first non-Japanese CEO of the Olympus group, the well-known Japanese camera and optical equipment manufacturer. Woodford, a 'down-to-earth' British businessman who speaks no Japanese, was not a very obvious choice for the job; according to *FACTA*, a Japanese magazine, the company had 'picked a bottom-ranking foreign executive director with virtually no significant responsibilities from amongst a total pool of 25 potential candidates, including the vice-president who was responsible for medical instruments ...'.

Woodford, who had been made President and COO in April, had been passed a translation of *FACTA* magazine articles in the summer of 2011 that alleged a number of serious irregularities had occurred at Olympus.

- The purchase of three companies between 2006 and 2008 for $910.6 billion. None of these companies had a turnover in excess of $2.6 million, and the acquisition costs were written off without explanation.

- The 2008 purchase of Gyrus, a UK medical equipment firm, allegedly at a grossly inflated price.

◆ Most of Olympus's acquisitions – many of which were unsuccessful – had been handled by Global Company, a firm that was alleged to have had an overly close relationship with Olympus.

◆ A massive foreign currency loss of $1.3 billion for the year ending March 2011.

Woodford conscientiously attempted to make enquiries about the article's claims, but was stonewalled by the Chairman of Olympus, Tsuyoshi Kikukawa, and the Executive Vice-president Hisashi Mori, among others. In late September *FACTA* published its October issue, which contained more damaging allegations about Olympus. Woodford demanded to be made CEO, believing that this would give him sufficient authority to conduct a proper internal investigation. The company agreed, but at a board meeting on 30 September it was plain to Woodford that other board members were not cooperating.

Flying to London, Woodford instructed the major auditing firm PricewaterhouseCoopers (PWC) to investigate. PWC produced a report quickly that found Olympus had lost $1,287 million in 'shareholder value' in a series of unsuccessful acquisitions and other investments. Woodford sent the PWC report to Kikukawa and Mori, demanding their resignations. Three days later Woodford was fired, and Kikukawa resumed the positions of President and CEO. Woodford then reported Olympus to the UK's Serious Fraud Office.

The cat was out of the bag. Kikukawa soon had to resign, was arrested, and is currently on trial for falsifying accounts. He has pleaded guilty, but what had really happened? The answer is obscure, and is yet to be fully explained. Back in the 1980s, when Japan was enjoying a massive economic bubble, the US had arranged the Plaza Accord, a deal with other major economies to depreciate the US dollar against the Japanese yen and German mark. This had led to massive drop in Olympus's income after 1985 as the price of its products had become higher in the vital American market. According to an internal report, Olympus then embarked on 'aggressive financial asset management', which suffered massive losses when the Japanese bubble burst in 1990. That year the company had to hide losses of 100 billion yen (then worth approximately $730 million). The losses in 'financial instruments' (the report does not give details of what these were) continued to grow, and the firm apparently took steps to disguise and/or defer booking the losses, in the hope that other, more risky investments would generate profits to compensate.

Since the burst of its economic bubble in 1990, corporate Japan, once the terror of less efficient Western industries, has been in the doldrums. As we are often told, Japanese business is different; it is notoriously difficult for foreigners to penetrate the inner workings of Japanese firms, and observers are not optimistic that the ongoing court cases involving Olympus will reveal the full story of what occurred. The consensus at present is that the irregularities at Olympus, such as the ridiculously expensive acquisitions and massive finder's fees paid by the company, occurred as part of a process of hiding large losses inherited from the 1980s. There are also persistent claims that Olympus had paid large sums to the Yakuza, the Japanese mafia, over the years.

Olympus is not some obscure Far Eastern outfit. It is a long-established firm (founded in 1919) with global brands, and produces excellent, high-quality products. As well as being a leading digital camera manufacturer, it controls 70% of the global market for gastro-intestinal endoscopes, worth $2.5 billion. It is almost 30% foreign-owned, and with numerous subsidiaries established in the West, so the scandal has attracted the interest of the authorities in the US and the UK, including the SEC, the FBI and the Serious Fraud Office.

Japan is, in many respects, a developed 'Western' economy. It is a major embarrassment for Japan that a foreign CEO blew the whistle on one of the country's most important firms. However, it is not clear if the Japanese authorities are prepared to introduce adequate reforms. For example, an attempt during 2012 to introduce a requirement that all listed firms have at least one external director was quashed – but as Olympus did indeed have several external directors who do not appear to have played a significant role in uncovering the fraud, such a measure might not have been effective in any case. According to Jamie Allen, of the Asian Corporate Governance Association, 'Olympus does reflect many of the problems of corporate governance in Japan that people have been talking about for years ... Whilst not every company may be as bad as this, I certainly don't think Olympus is an isolated case in terms of its overall weak corporate governance system.' The Japan Business Federation, known as the 'Keidanren', a powerful organisation with 1600 member companies that is widely regarded as the voice of big business, appears to be strongly resistant to any reforms. While the country's ruling party, the Democratic Party of Japan, came to power in 2009 promising reforms in corporate governance, little has been achieved so far (perhaps partly due to other crises in Japan, such as the 2011 earthquake and tsunami).

It should not be news to investors that Japan has weak corporate governance. The explanations usually offered relate to the country's culture. As well as the well-known aversion to 'losing face' (being humiliated), there are strong tendencies not only to keep problems quiet and try to fix them privately (as appears to have occurred in the case of Olympus) but also to close ranks, especially in the face of foreign criticism. This is generally blamed on 'Old Japan' or the 'Old Guard', but it is not at all clear that there is any 'New Guard' emerging capable of implementing genuine reforms.

In light of this, the much vaunted purchase of approximately 11.5% of Olympus by Sony that was agreed in late 2012 does little to reassure. Sony, which has been making losses for four years, is as much part of 'Old Japan' as Olympus. Sony's injection of $645 million into Olympus will help stave off immediate problems, and there are, no doubt, elements of synergy – for example, Sony makes image sensors for Olympus's endoscopes – that may bring some tangible benefits for the two firms, but not enough to justify the investment. Foreign shareholders, in particular, are concerned that Sony will be buying newly issued shares from Olympus, which may, depending on the final details, dilute the value of existing shareholdings. Critics see the whole affair as emblematic of the way 'Old Japan' protects its own, and predict that little will be done to prevent similar episodes in the future – the company, remember, fraudulently hid massive losses for nearly two decades.

The man who became the 'Man from Del Monte'

The story of Polly Peck, a small UK clothes manufacturer that grew rapidly into an international conglomerate and becoming a constituent of the FTSE100 (the *Financial Times* index of the top 100 UK-listed companies) before collapsing in 1990, illustrates an important point for investors: it *is* possible to make money by investing in a company with fraudulent accounts. If you had got in to Polly Peck in the early 1980s and had sold your shares shortly before the collapse, you could have made a return of more than 1,000%, not bad for holding an investment for less than a decade. This is the temptation underlying the 'bigger fool' method of investment, where you make an investment in the hope that a bigger fool than you will eventually take the shares off your hands at a higher price.

In 1980 Polly Peck had been listed on the London stock market for several years, but it was very small and didn't seem to be heading anywhere exciting. Then a dynamic young businessman named Asil Nadir, a Turkish Cypriot, purchased 58% of Polly Peck for £270,000, and everything began to change. Becoming CEO of Polly Peck in July, he immediately launched a rights issue, successfully raising £1.5 million. This cash enabled him to begin an aggressive programme of growth.

The first place that Nadir looked for opportunities was in Northern Cyprus, a territory that had been set up with the help of Turkey during ethnic troubles on the island in the 1970s. The Turkish Federated State of Cyprus, as it was then called, was not recognised internationally and was suffering a trade embargo. It was in dire need of economic stimulus, and Nadir spotted potential in the citrus industry and in tourism. Over the next few years Nadir was, allegedly, able to obtain commercial buildings, development land and large expanses of citrus plantations at very low cost from the Turkish Cypriot authorities, which were eager to put these properties, many of which had been abandoned by Greek Cypriot owners during the troubles of the previous decade, to productive use. Here was a local son who had made good in London returning to try to help his own homeland in its time of need – it was, in other words, probably far less sinister a series of deals than has often been suggested. Nadir set up three companies in Cyprus: Uni-Pac packaging, SunZest Trading and Voyager Kibris. Uni-Pac was a cardboard box manufacturer, essential for any serious efforts at citrus exporting from Cyprus and Turkey, SunZest handled the fruit, and Voyager Kibris was a tourism company that purchased a Sheraton hotel in mainland Turkey and began to develop hotel sites in Northern Cyprus.

In 1982 Nadir purchased control of another small UK-listed firm, Cornell Dresses, through which he raised further capital, set up a mineral water bottler, Niksar, in Turkey, and in 1984 entered into a joint venture, Vestel, with the British firm Thorn-EMI, to manufacture televisions and other electrical goods. While still under Nadir's control Vestel became one of the main profit centres for the Polly Peck group, and today both Niksar and Vestel have grown into substantial international brands. Although seemingly a dangerously eclectic collection of businesses, they were in fact well-chosen to exploit the political and economic conditions in Turkey and Northern Cyprus; colour television, for example, only came to Turkey in 1984 and there was a huge demand for low-cost TVs).

Everything depended, however, on the confidence of the City of London. Nadir had a good track record, having built up his own small listed firm, Wearwell, in East London during the 1970s, establishing clothes manufacturing facilities in Northern Cyprus, where labour was cheap. He was also charming and charismatic. Better still, the time was right: under Margaret Thatcher, 'UK plc' was expanding and optimistic, enjoying a bonanza as State-owned industries were privatised, generating large profits for stock market intermediaries and bringing a new generation of British investors into the stock market. During the early 1980s, Nadir looked like the kind of dynamic entrepreneur who was wanted in the UK, and his interest in Turkey and Turkish Cyprus, never well-understood in the City, looked like a proposition that, although risky, might pay off big time. By 1983, 85% of the shares not controlled by Asil Nadir were owned by UK financial institutions.

There were, of course, dissident voices. Critics pointed out that the Northern Cyprus ventures, in particular, were acutely vulnerable to political developments – what would happen if, for example, the island was re-unified? Polly Peck had obtained special permission from the Stock Exchange to exclude a breakdown by territory (normally required) in its accounts, which made it impossible for investors to figure out how much money was being made in each country in which the group was active.

But Polly Peck was growing fast, and investors, sensibly, tend to like growth. Its 1982 accounts showed more than three times growth in sales on the previous year, with the bulk of the profits coming from the citrus operations. Significantly, the textile side of the business was making a loss. There had been questions about the high margins that Polly Peck was earning on its fruit; Nadir gave one of the standard explanations used by conglomerates, namely that the vertical integration of the business (growing, packing, transporting and wholesaling) had produced cost-saving synergies and hence higher profits. Although the share price dropped badly on fears that Turkey might remove what were believed to be valuable tax concessions, it recovered and continued its upward trajectory.

In 1984 Cornell Dresses and Wearwell were merged into the Polly Peck group, and for the first time Polly Peck revalued its real estate, giving it a reserve of £8 million which helped to offset exchange rate losses. With the exception of 1985, Polly Peck then revalued its real estate each year until it collapsed. The turnover and profit picture, however, was very rosy. Turnover had grown from £1 million in 1980 to £6.5 million in 1981, £21.1 million in 1982, £62.2 million in 1983, £137.2 million in 1984, and £205.5 million in 1985, with profits after tax during the same period rising steadily each year from a small loss in 1980 to a very healthy £50.5 million in 1985.

With institutional money behind it, Polly Peck just seemed to go from strength to strength. Vestel obtained licences to manufacture for major international electronics firms such as Akai. The group bought British home appliance maker Russell Hobbs and Taiwanese electronics firm Capetronic in 1987, and enjoyed a substantial share price rise in the same year, due in part to it becoming available to US investors for the first time (via specialist mutual funds and 'American Depositary Receipts' (ADRs), an instrument that allows Americans to invest directly in approved foreign firms). In 1988 it continued to expand, buying companies and setting up joint ventures in Hong Kong, the US, Holland and Spain, acquiring ten refrigerated ships and nearly doubling its assets. In 1989, at the height of the leveraged buyout boom (see Chapter 2) the US firm RJR Nabisco, itself the product of a very heavily leveraged merger, needed to sell a valuable asset, and decided to put the well-known food company, Del Monte, up for sale. Polly Peck bought Del Monte for $875 million (£575 million), making it the third-largest fruit wholesaler in the world. In the same year, it purchased Sansui, an electronics manufacturer listed on the Tokyo Stock Exchange, as well as a host of smaller firms, and was included for the first time in the FTSE 100 Index. In slightly less than a decade, Polly Peck's market capitalisation had grown from £300,000 to $1.7 billion, a staggering achievement for a UK-based firm. Nadir himself was now listed as the 36th richest person in the UK.

In hindsight it may seem obvious that there must have been something funny about such rapid growth, but at the time this was less obvious. Not long after it became known in late 1990 that a Serious Fraud Office investigation had begun, the *New York Times*, usually fairly reliable, opined that 'the Polly Peck business appears to be sound'. In early August Nadir announced his intention to buy back Polly Peck's shares in the market (he already owned 25%) and turn it into a private company. The share price rose from 393p to 417p on the news, despite reports that the Inland Revenue was investigating the group for insider trading. Five days later, on 17 August, Nadir announced that he was abandoning the bid, precipitating a change of attitude in the City. Within weeks, the SFO had raided the offices of South Audley Management, a company that handled Nadir's private dealings, banks holding Nadir's Polly Peck shares against loans they had made to him began to sell them off quietly, the group's shares had collapsed and been suspended from trading on the stock market, the company was put into administration and it was becoming clear that there would be a sustained effort in Turkey and Northern Cyprus to obstruct any efforts by the UK authorities to examine the books of Polly Peck's subsidiaries in those jurisdictions.

The catalyst for the collapse was Nadir's rapid retraction of his bid to make the group private (breaking Stock Exchange rules), but it is still unclear why he chose to announce the bid in the first place. Some knowledgeable insiders suggest that it may somehow be related to the Gulf War, which had begun on 2 August 1990 and had severely disrupted business in Turkey, which has a border with Iraq, as well as with other Middle East markets. Others have suggested that it was somehow related to insider trading, but investigations into this have produced no tangible results. Yet others have pointed out that Nadir was frustrated at the low price to earnings ratio of the group, which during 1990 was about 8 – a reasonable level, given the dangers of overexpansion for a group that was growing mainly by acquisition. The company itself claimed, on 1 October, that it was the share price collapse following Nadir's retraction of his bid that had provoked a liquidity crisis in the company; there are strong suspicions, however, that the group had had frequent liquidity crises during the years of expansion.

Whatever the reason, once Polly Peck was in administration many problems began to appear. A substantial part of the value in Polly Peck was supposed to be in the Turkish and Cypriot subsidiaries, but in October a Turkish banker stated that 'Mr Nadir is not succeeding in selling anything here ... He has no way out now.' For investors and lenders, the most urgent issue was to establish how much money was in the Near Eastern subsidiaries that might be recovered, but auditors were still unable to gain access to their accounts, owing to court injunctions and in some cases, outright refusal. Attention turned to Polly Peck's accountants, the first line of defence against corporate governance failures and it was becoming abundantly clear that there were serious corporate governance failures at Polly Peck. The group's Chief Accountant, John Turner, was expelled from the Institute of Chartered Accountants in 1998, having admitted to his involvement in 'inappropriate transactions' and the 'preparation of inaccurate documents'. Turner admitted ten charges relating to transfers of money from the UK to Polly Peck subsidiaries abroad. Sir John Bailey, Chairman of the tribunal, said that Turner's behaviour was like 'clapping the glass to the sightless eye'. Stoy Hayward, Polly Peck's external accountants, got off lightly, receiving a fine of only £75,000 years later, in 2002, when it admitted a number of complaints mostly relating to failures in monitoring the work of secondary auditors in Cyprus. In 2003 three accountants at the secondary auditors in Cyprus, Erdal & Co., were fined and reprimanded by the UK's Accountants' Joint Disciplinary Scheme for having provided audits of the Cypriot subsidiaries to Stoy Hayward that 'bore no relationship to reality'. For the investors and lenders it was all much, much too late.

The Polly Peck debacle also had a political dimension. Nadir had contributed some £440,000 to the Conservative Party, a sum that opponents are currently demanding be repaid. After Nadir fled to Northern Cyprus in 1993 to escape trial in the UK, Michael Mates, Northern Ireland Minister, resigned after having tried to defend Nadir against the investigations. Much has been made of Mates's gift of a £50 watch to Nadir with the inscription 'Don't let the buggers get you down' – a little inappropriate, perhaps, but hardly an extreme of wickedness. Because of Northern Cyprus's peculiar international status there was no extradition treaty, and Asil Nadir was able to live there in style without fear of UK prosecution, a fact that enraged investors and commentators in the UK. In 2010, 17 years after he had escaped to Cyprus, Asil Nadir returned to the UK to stand trial. In 2012 he was found guilty on ten specimen charges relating to the theft of £26.2 million from Polly Peck and was sentenced to ten years, of which, said the judge, he will serve only five.

So why did Nadir return? Part of the reason must be the changed situation in Turkey, the economy of which has developed substantially and now is under enormous pressure to conform to Western standards in business. With his fortune dwindling, Nadir seems to have lost political support in Northern Cyprus, too. It's embarrassing to harbour a fugitive businessman when you are trying to become more respectable yourself. Furthermore, Nadir's persistent suggestions that he was somehow victimised in the UK for being ethnically Turkish seems to have worn increasingly thin among Turks and Turkish Cypriots themselves. Enforced exile in rural Northern Cyprus, though pleasant enough, had become frustrating for a man who loved the cosmopolitan high life, according to reports, and Nadir's inability to travel internationally (for fear of extradition to the UK) had become intolerable, but these factors do not provide the whole answer. One possibility is that Nadir misinterpreted the messages emanating from the UK, and thought he would be exonerated at the trial. Another is that he was deliberately misled by unknown parties into believing this. Perhaps he thought that now the Conservatives were back in power he would get better treatment. He certainly seems to have been genuinely surprised at the verdict.

In recent years Polly Peck has become a case study for business students, and great emphasis has been laid on the group's 'currency mismatching'. In Polly Peck's case, currency mismatching meant borrowing in strong currencies like the pound and the Swiss franc at low rates of interest and investing it in territories using soft currencies like the Turkish lira at high rates of return. This had the effect of bolstering the profit and loss account while driving down the balance sheet. In the present writer's view, however, this is not the crux of the wrongdoing at Polly Peck. The crucial point is that British accountants and auditors were willing to accept false information emanating from Polly Peck's subsidiaries in Turkey and Northern Cyprus during the 1980s, and investors in the UK (and later the US) relied upon these assurances.

> The crucial point is that British accountants and auditors were willing to accept false information emanating from Polly Peck's subsidiaries in Turkey and Northern Cyprus during the 1980s, and investors in the UK (and later the US) relied upon these assurances.

They had to, given that Turkey and Turkish Cyprus are not well understood in the UK. This was a serious failure of the accounting profession in the UK, and although it led to the Cadbury Report, which attempted to raise standards of corporate governance, investors cannot have total confidence in the value of audits, especially in situations involving subsidiaries in countries that don't work on the Anglo-Saxon model of business (see page 156).

Investors versus business shamans

From a private investor's perspective, the shenanigans at Olympus and Polly Peck are less serious than many of the other cases discussed in this book, not least because few investors can have thought it appropriate to sink their entire wealth into a single company. More importantly, the underlying businesses were solid, not fictional as in the cases of Madoff and Stanford. Olympus makes great products for which there is worldwide demand. Polly Peck's businesses were mostly sound, and some of them, such as Vestel, the TV manufacturer, have prospered greatly since Polly Peck's collapse. In Olympus's case the wrongdoing relates to the concealment of losses incurred during the really excessive Japanese bubble of the 1980s when most, if not all, large Japanese firms committed egregious investment errors. This was compounded by Olympus's 'financial engineering', the details of which have not been revealed. The executives who maintained the cover-up for so many years do not appear to have done so for personal gain, but out of loyalty to the company and their predecessors. Since the Japanese bubble burst UK investors have generally been advised to avoid Japan, with its countless 'zombie companies' receiving continuous government bailouts or unable to repay their debts, its 'Lost Decade' of the 1990s and its continuing dire need for more corporate transparency. It would have taken a brave private investor in the UK, therefore, to have decided to take a punt directly on Olympus or any other large Japanese firm.

The attractions of Polly Peck were rather greater for British investors. It was a creature of its time, when a pro-business government was trying to encourage the general public to invest in the stock market. The ethos in the City of London was short-termist and somewhat cynical – the financial institutions that backed Polly Peck may well have been operating on the 'bigger fool theory', as has often been suggested, and to have placed less faith in the accuracy of the company's accounts than did the small investors who followed them in. But in those days, even private investors often regarded short-termism as the only sensible way to invest – you got into a company that had the political and commercial wind behind it, and hoped to get out before anything went wrong – and for nearly a decade nothing did go wrong. While this is not a sound way to manage your entire portfolio, it is not entirely unreasonable to do this with a small proportion of it (see Chapter 12). This may sound like a rather amoral attitude, but successful investors do sometimes allow themselves to practise a little judicious opportunism, and take a risk on a booming firm whose accounts are less than ideal. If they lose out, of course, they really cannot put all of the blame on others.

PART THREE

Why we get the swindlers we deserve

7

Some deadly sins of investment: trusting false prophets, investing for the Apocalypse and the money illusion

Is the person you seek advice from able to give you a credible answer?

Robert Kiyosaki, personal finance guru

So far, this book has dealt mainly with the misdeeds of fraudsters. Now we should turn our attention to some of the faults that we ourselves as investors often commit. Perhaps the cardinal sin is ignorance: private investors really do need to educate themselves about investment, and to continue to do this for their entire investing lives. It is important to be careful about where you get your investment education from. Anyone who tells you that investing is a sure thing, or who provides vague, oversimplified guidance for what are often complex issues is unlikely to be a useful source of knowledge – so be discriminating.

In this chapter we will examine three common investment 'sins': following a charismatic investment guru, being overly attached to gold, and the 'money illusion' (an economic term that refers to confusion between nominal and inflation-adjusted figures).

All of these sins leave investors potentially vulnerable to fraud, but even when there is no fraud they can lead to serious investment blunders.

Selling the sizzle, not the steak

In 1997 Robert Kiyosaki, a former salesman from Hawaii, self-published a book entitled *Rich Dad, Poor Dad*. It is written in the form of parables, a specific genre in self-help books employed by such runaway successes as *Who Moved My Cheese?* After gaining popularity in multilevel marketing circles, the book was picked up by a mainstream publisher and went on to be a best-seller, leading to a book series (total sales for the series are claimed to be in excess of 20 million copies), including *Why We Want You To Be Rich: Two Men, One Message*, a title co-authored with Donald Trump, the lugubrious real estate tycoon. From unpromising beginnings, Kiyosaki became an international celebrity (he was even hyped on Oprah Winfrey's television show in 2000) with a strong business in motivational seminars. *Rich Dad, Poor Dad* has become, *Time* magazine has claimed, 'the number one personal finance book in the history of the world'.

The central message of *Rich Dad, Poor Dad* is that if you want to be rich, you should adopt the attitudes of Kiyosaki's 'rich dad', the father of a school friend who had become rich without the benefit of higher education. What you should not do, according to the book, is to imitate the outlook of Kiyosaki's own father, 'poor dad', a respectable school superintendent in Hawaii who is depicted in the book as lacking in entrepreneurial spirit. Instead of working hard and saving, Kiyosaki recommends that you acquire income-producing assets. This boils down mostly to buying rental properties or starting an unspecified business.

I have a sneaking sympathy for some self-help books, but not for this one: in my view it is largely gibberish. Kiyosaki flits distractedly from one topic to the next in a cloud of slogans and clichés. There is little concrete advice, and what there is consists partly of erroneous statements (for example, on the US tax deductibility of certain personal expenses), and unverifiable claims (such as that Kiyosaki has made many millions in a diverse set of businesses), and he even advocates potentially illegal activities such as insider trading (see Chapter 2). Mostly, though, it poses as an inspirational book, clearly aimed at people with low incomes and not much education – hence its repetitive message that you do not need to have a high income or a good education to get rich. This is, of course, true, but not quite in the way that Kiyosaki is insinuating, and certainly not often at a very high speed.

Normally personal finance gurus who aim at this market do not receive much attention in the mainstream media. They may make a comfortable living catering to the aspirations of some vulnerable people, but they have little or no influence on society at large, or on private investors in particular. But this is not to do justice to Kiyosaki: he is 'huge'. *Rich Dad, Poor Dad* and two of his other titles managed to reach number one on the best-seller lists of the *Wall Street Journal* and the *New York Times*, as well as in other countries around the world. He is a financial columnist and 'expert' on Yahoo finance. He has appeared many times on television, and his book has been endorsed by film stars such as Will Smith. And there is his association with the real estate tycoon Donald Trump, with whom he has co-authored the book *Why We Want You To Be Rich*.

Robert Kiyosaki matters because Robert Kiyosaki is famous, and famous people have influence. Although he claims to be committed to financial education, his books contain little useful financial education and much that is inadequate or misleading. There is nothing wrong in principle with, for instance, advocating entrepreneurship, or with suggesting that money can be made in property, but Kiyosaki does not provide adequate guidance on how to deal with the nitty gritty in these fields; his books are 'inspirational' and general, rather than practical and specific.

Investigations into Kiyosaki's background have revealed connections between the financial guru and a number of cult-like multilevel marketing organisations and self-help organisations. For a start, Kiyosaki agrees that in

1974 he underwent training at EST that, he says, was life-changing. EST, short for Erhard Seminars Training, was a New Age seminar organisation in the 1970s and 1980s that became controversial because of its confrontational methods. Its founder, Werner Erhard, told a *Financial Times* reporter in 2012 that 'I'm not nice. I don't say nice things. I don't like nice people ... I find being nice is committed to me, not to you', which gives a flavour of the kind of material dished out at these seminars. In the 1980s Kiyosaki joined a programme called 'Money and You' that had been established by another EST alumnus, Marshall Thurber. In 1984 Kiyosaki and others took the programme to Australia, running it successfully for nearly a decade. Then, in 1993, an Australian news show *Four Corners* ran a critical piece on 'Money and You' that included interviews with people who had attended the seminars. According to one attendee, 'we got to a stage where virtually everybody in the hall at one stage was crying ... Some of them were on the verge of a nervous breakdown ... You start losing sight of your own values and your own convictions.' This is reminiscent of descriptions of the EST weekends that were held back in the 1970s. The *Four Corners* report was apparently damaging to 'Money and You' in Australia, and in the following year Kiyosaki left the organisation for unrelated reasons, according to him.

Kiyosaki has also had a relationship with Amway, a direct selling organisation that uses multilevel marketing (MLM) techniques to purvey beauty, health and cleaning products around the world. MLM, which has been heavily criticised, rewards its salespeople not only for the products they manage to sell, but also for the new salespeople they recruit. Although the MLM company itself and the more successful salespeople may make money in MLM, many other sale recruits may not, often being required to pay in substantial funds to obtain their stock and get started. According to a 2011 report, active Amway distributors were earning only $115 a month on average. David Bromley, a sociologist of religion, describes Amway as a 'quasi-religious corporation' in which successful Amway distributors can 'receive lucrative fees for speaking at Amway seminars and rallies'. In the US, participants at Amway meetings are often presented with a strong message that Americans have lost touch with the personal qualities which allegedly made America great, and by selling Amway products they can become successful self-employed businesspeople. Bromley compares the meetings with the old-fashioned religious revival meetings, with individuals shouting out affirmations such as 'I believe!' and 'How sweet it is!' during speeches and award presentations. Politically, Amway seems to be very conservative, which appears to reflect the beliefs of the types of people who want to become distributors. A very powerful element in Amway's appeal is that, like a cult, it provides a kind of ersatz family, a group structure that provides much emotional support to its members.

So how close is Kiyosaki's connection with Amway? It is claimed that an Amway executive found a copy of the original self-published version of *Rich Dad, Poor Dad* and adopted it as an aid to enthusiasm for Amway distributors, giving the book the boost it needed to be adopted by a mainstream publisher, as mentioned above. It is further claimed that Kiyosaki was at one time an Amway distributor, although he appears not to have made any public statements on this matter. It is certainly the case that Amway participants have used Kiyosaki's material to support Amway's advocacy of being your own boss, and Kiyosaki himself has endorsed network marketing (a type of MLM) in his book *The Business of the 21st Century.*

Americans, we are told, are used to being sold at, and are fairly immune to the hard sell, although to judge by his book sales, they are not all immune to Kiyosaki. Kiyosaki-related products and seminars are being sold around the world, reaching people in developing countries who do not really understand how the modern, Western-style world works: everything Western looks shiny and wonderful to them, which is distressing to those of us who know better.

While writing this section I was startled to hear from an affluent Chinese Singaporean friend that she had recently attended a Kiyosaki talk in Singapore. Singapore is not a developing country – in many ways it is one of the most advanced countries in the world – but beneath its modern surface lurk cultural attitudes that, to Western eyes, seem curiously credulous.

My friend, who should know better, really could not tell the difference between Kiyosaki's discourse and that of a credible investor with a proven track record like Jim Rogers, an erstwhile partner of George Soros who now lives in Singapore. My friend also tends to commit the other investment sins discussed below, which reminds me that it is not only the poor and the vulnerable who are liable to make such mistakes. The point here is really that 'inspiration' from a guru is no substitute for genuine financial education, which takes years to acquire; if you are starting out as an investor and don't know much, read as many financial books as you can, as well as the high-end financial press, and don't rely on any single person (present author included) to tell you how things 'really' are.

Gold bugs: waiting for Armageddon

There are people on this earth who believe that certain metals, usually gold, are a better long- term store of value than anything else. They are entitled to their opinion, but they do not hold this view in the same way that someone else might believe, say, that residential property in the UK has been a good investment during the last 50 years. They believe it with a fiery, dogmatic passion that is almost mystical. They despise 'fiat' money (money created by governments that is not fixed in value). They refuse to consider all aspects of the problem; non-gold bugs are regarded as wilfully ignorant at best, and as running dogs of a conspiracy of the rich, at worst.

> There are people on this earth who believe that certain metals, usually gold, are a better long-term store of value than anything else.

They trash any dissident view, even if it is expressed by a Nobel Prize winning economist, like Paul Krugman, or a well-regarded top investor like Warren Buffett.

In his shareholders letter of 2011, Buffett makes the important point that gold is a type of asset which never produces a return, and argues people only buy it in the hope the price will go up (this isn't always true, since some eccentric people appear to buy gold with the sole expectation it will be the only store of value when the imminent collapse of modern society finally occurs). He accepts the gold bugs' contention that we cannot trust governments to prevent the gradual dilution of the value of fiat money through inflation, but he does not believe we should therefore put all our money in gold. According to Buffett, the world's extracted gold store currently totals approximately 170,000 metric tonnes, which would form a cube with sides of 68 feet and be worth, at the market price in 2011, $9.6 trillion. He then compares this gigantic gold cube with other investments you could purchase for $9.6 trillion. This second collection could include *all* US cropland (400 million acres producing $200 billion a year) plus 16 companies of the size of the world's most profitable firm, Exxon Mobil, which generates $40 billion a year, and you would still have $1 trillion left over. On this analysis, no investor with $9.6 trillion would put it all in gold, which produces nothing, when he or she could invest it productively in assets that could produce $840 billion each year and still be valuable saleable assets in the future.

These are strong arguments to a reasonable person, but they leave the more extreme gold bugs unmoved. Their main problem is fear: fear that an irresponsible government will lead the country into hyperinflation; and a fear civilisation will collapse. In such a scenario, they argue, gold will be the only thing between you and penury. This seems rather unlikely for a number of reasons, not least that the authorities can be expected to try to take all your gold from you in such a scenario. Also, in the event of a collapse so apocalyptic that there is a total breakdown in law and order, how exactly do you think you are going to protect your gold from bandits, even if you are a survivalist lunatic with a bunker and some guns? To see why holding gold is not necessarily a good hedge against social chaos, let's consider very briefly two real-life scenarios: the exodus of the Vietnamese boat people after the end of the Vietnam War, and the hyperinflation in Germany during the early 1920s.

After the fall of Saigon to the North Vietnamese in 1975, large numbers of Vietnamese sought to escape persecution by taking boats and putting out to sea in the hope of reaching a safe haven. It is estimated that between

200,000 and 400,000 people died at sea, through accidents and piracy. Some individuals had bought their way on to these boats with exorbitant amounts of gold. Then, in 1979, following harassment and expropriations, the Vietnamese authorities agreed to permit ethnic Chinese to leave the country if they wanted. To obtain a permit, you had to pay several ounces of gold, per person, to the Public Security Bureau. It is estimated that $115 million (2.5% of the country's GNP) was extracted in this way. The lesson? Having some gold might just save your life in an escape, but you might have trouble taking a lot of it with you, owing to its weight and the danger of robbery and expropriation.

The well-known Weimar hyperinflation occurred during a two-and-a-half-year period in Germany between June 1921 and January 1924. The catalyst was the requirement that Germany pay war reparations in gold or foreign currency to the victorious powers in the Great War; Germany had to purchase large amounts of foreign currency, which had the effect of causing the German mark to fall in value rapidly, raising prices dramatically at home. The effects of the hyperinflation were felt differently by different socio-economic classes: for example, initially workers were paid more frequently, with larger and larger sums of paper money, and were still able to obtain food; the middle classes, relying on savings, suffered dramatic drops in the value of their assets and were quickly reduced to penury, especially if they sold their houses to raise cash. People who had borrowed large sums earlier, on the other hand, did well, since they could repay their debts easily in devalued marks. One of the most unpleasant effects of the inflation was that, although there was plenty of food available in the countryside, farmers refused to sell it for marks and towns and cities were starved of food. Even if you had some gold or foreign currency, it was hard to get food in the towns; in Breslau, for instance, one foreigner found that he could only obtain 'one square meal a day by crowding into a restaurant in the early morning and waiting until luncheon was served some hours later'. Malnutrition was particularly severe among children. Inevitably, by autumn 1923 the government had given itself powers to seize foreign currency, gold and other precious metals, and to open post and break into people's houses to find them. In Berlin there were police raids on cafés during which café customers were forced to hand over any foreign currency in their wallets.

Having some gold – a gold chain, say, or some gold coins – might have helped you to obtain essentials, but in Germany other valuables such as grand pianos, good paintings, and even cigars were also used. In neither Germany nor Vietnam did gold provide complete safety. Thus the belief that holding all your assets in gold will protect you in dire circumstances is probably an illusion.

So does this mean that investors should hold no gold? Perhaps not; some experts recommend holding a small proportion, say 5%, of your financial assets in gold. Taking transaction costs into consideration, the cheapest way to do this is to hold bullion in a specialist gold vault, if you can afford it, but this is unlikely to be a good solution to the problem of how to pay for things if cash won't buy them – you may not be able to physically take possession of your bullion in a major crisis, and even if you can, shaving bits of gold off your gold bars to buy things may attract some very unwelcome attention. This is not a book on how to survive a violent social collapse, but wise investors should give some thought to how they can plan for such an undesirable event. Experience suggests that a spread of assets, some easily moveable and tradeable, like jewellery, and some not, like buildings and land, may help, but they will not on their own provide a guarantee of anything – but neither will holing up in a cellar with an assault weapon and a pile of gold. If the apocalypse ever occurs, all bets will be off.

The money illusion

In 1922 the celebrated American economist Irving Fisher went to Germany to investigate attitudes among Germans during the hyperinflation. One woman he spoke to, a Berlin shopkeeper, sold him a shirt. 'Fearing to be thought a profiteer, she said: "That shirt I sold you will cost me just as much to replace as I am charging you." Before I could ask her why, then, she sold it at so low a price, she continued: "But I have made a profit on that shirt because I bought it for less."' According to Fisher, the woman was wrong: she had in fact made a loss in real terms. The sum he paid for the shirt, 150 marks, was, according to his calculations, only worth 90 1921 marks (he doesn't say exactly when in 1921), and since the cost price to the woman had been 100 1921 marks, she had lost the equivalent of 10 1921 marks. This, says Fisher, was the result of the 'money illusion', the inability to distinguish clearly between the nominal value of currency and its 'real', or inflation-adjusted, value. Fisher believed that the money illusion occurs because people tend to think of their own currency as fixed in value and of all other things as fluctuating in price.

There is clearly something in this idea, although it remains a topic of vigorous debate among academic economists.

On the most basic level, it is the case that many people, even if they are vaguely aware of the effects of inflation, aren't very good at calculating inflation adjustments, or, indeed, at spotting when nominal and real figures are being confused. For example, politicians and journalists frequently commit these errors, while financial services firms are not above quoting rates of return in nominal terms without mentioning the fact unless regulations prevent them from doing so. Consider the following statement from the UK Prime Minister David Cameron in a 2010 speech: 'And here I want to say something to the people who got us into this mess. The ones who racked up more debt in 13 years than previous governments did in three centuries. Yes you, Labour.' While it may be true that the Labour Party did not manage the economy very well during those 13 years, Cameron's statement was deeply misleading because he was talking about a nominal increase in debt; if all the figures were expressed in inflation-adjusted terms, Labour's debt would look considerably smaller when compared with the three centuries of debt to which Cameron referred.

> On the most basic level, it is the case that many people, even if they are vaguely aware of the effects of inflation, aren't very good at calculating inflation adjustments, or, indeed, at spotting when nominal and real figures are being confused.

In the housing market, the money illusion seems to have a bearing on price bubbles. Suppose a young couple is trying to decide whether to buy or rent. They can obtain a permanently fixed-rate mortgage. They assume that real and nominal interest rates move in tandem (they don't). If inflation is decreasing, they may think that buying a house is cheaper than renting, failing to take into account that decreasing inflation will increase the cost of future mortgage payments in real terms. If they, and many like them, decide to buy, house prices will be forced upwards. Furthermore, nominal house prices are 'sticky' in a market downturn. People don't want to sell their houses for less than what they paid for them in nominal terms, even if they could purchase another house more cheaply than they could have done earlier. If someone purchases a flat for, say, £100,000 and prices drop by 5%, the tendency is to hold out for the nominal purchase price even if they can now buy a similar flat for £95,000. This tendency has the effect of drastically reducing the volume of transactions, making the market stagnate.

Much depends upon the presentation, or 'framing', of an issue. For instance, there is experimental evidence that when offered a choice between a 2% wage increase at a time of 4% inflation and a 2% wage cut at a time of 0% inflation, people will tend to prefer the former, even though there is no difference in the loss in real terms. A nominal increase just seems to be better. If the question is framed in a different way that emphasises the effects in real terms, more people will see that there is no difference between the two in real terms.

Going back to the Berlin woman who sold Irving Fisher a shirt in 1922, it is noticeable that she was eager to emphasise the cost price of shirts had now risen to the retail price she was asking – in other words, the replacement cost of her stock had risen. This highlights the phenomenon that shoppers generally regard shopkeepers who sell old stock at new, higher prices during inflationary periods as acting unfairly. The Berlin shopkeeper was concerned that the shopper might perceive her higher nominal profit as a form of gouging. In fact, Fisher argued, she was unaware she was making a loss in real terms, but even if she had been aware of this she might still have been sensitive to shoppers' money illusion that she was making too large a profit.

Most economic transactions are expressed in nominal terms because it is easy, and in the short term the calculations may not diverge much from the real figures. Most of us can't easily adjust for inflation every time we buy or sell something, and nor do we need to. But for any important investment decision we should certainly do our inflation sums, usually by using price indices. A clear explanation of how to do this is available in a 'Statistical Literacy Guide' published by the House of Commons (available at: **www. parliament.uk/briefing-papers/SN04944**).

You can fool some of the people all of the time ...

Back in the 1970s, personal growth cults were all the rage among the young, partly in response to the excesses and drug abuse of the hippy era of the 1960s. In the 1970s, there was a marked move away from hedonism to focus on 'alternative' lifestyles that were more constructive. Cults and communes of various kinds offered ways of living that, while completely different from Western norms, seemed to promise a cleaner, better existence. They were not all bad; many cultish ideas from the 1970s, such as the value of organic foods, the toleration of diversity, and the importance of environmentalism have now become thoroughly mainstream and are often endorsed by major political parties. The more religiose cults, such as the Hare Krishna movement (the International Society for Krishna Consciousness), who have been described as the Jehovah's Witnesses of Hinduism, helped many addicts to recover from drug addiction through a spartan regime of work, sparse diet and singing. Some cults had a decidedly Western persona, using a Western psychological framework to teach techniques that were supposed to make you, the individual, a more effective, powerful and persuasive person in normal life – and many people who spent time with these groups have gone on to become successful in business, notably in the sales arena, where personal communication and persuasion skills are so important. Being communicative and persuasive, however, does not necessarily make you someone who has the analytical and reasoning ability to develop sound judgement in investment, and current investors need to be aware that there are quite a number of individuals and organisations operating today in the personal finance arena who have a background in the cults of the 1970s, and still use their techniques. Approach them with caution!

Periodically we hear respectable economists arguing for a return to the gold standard, the heyday of which was between 1870 and the outbreak of the First World War. During that period many of the more developed countries issued paper money which had a fixed value in terms of gold, and was often freely convertible to gold. The debate is complex and highly controversial, and ultimately not much use to the private investor who has to get along in the world today, where governments issue fiat money that is not tied to gold. Personally I am persuaded by those who argue that reintroducing a gold standard would not solve anything much, and would certainly not prevent governments from finding ways to manipulate the value of money. Fiat money is a problem for investors because it reduces in value over time, so we have to invest in productive assets like businesses and buildings, rather than living off the interest from our government bonds, like the Victorian family described in Galsworthy's famous series of novels, *The Forsyte Saga*. So, beware of gold bugs and the promoters of gold as an investment; they are unlikely to lead you to a way of making a good return.

Lastly, we need to train ourselves to think always in terms of real (inflation-adjusted) returns, not nominal returns, especially over the long term. If you do this, you will rapidly realise that cash deposits and bond yields often generate negative returns in real terms, and you will be less impressed by the massive nominal profit you just made by selling your house. Adjusting for inflation helps you to tell friend from foe, too; people who always quote nominal figures at you in investment either don't know what they are doing or are deliberately attempting to mislead. We need to develop a sense of what is really valuable, and what is an increase in value, regardless of nominal prices. There is a lot to be said, too, for keeping it simple. Warren Buffett tells a story of an old man who had started out as an itinerant peddler and had built up a successful department store. When his son came to him with big plans for a financial shake-up of the business, the old man told him to go and look in a storeroom on the seventh floor. 'You'll find the old cart I pushed here when I came to this town forty years ago,' he said. 'Mark that down as capital. Everything else is profit!'

8

Moral hazard in the system

The process by which banks create money is so simple the mind is repelled.
J.K. Galbraith, economist

One of the chief ways in which investors fall victim to fraud is that they misperceive the risks of a given investment – often with a little help from the people selling that investment! Prestidigitation is rife in the markets, as financial services firms do their best to make their offerings seem as attractive as possible. As we have seen, investors suffer from what economists call the 'principal–agent problem', where the investor is the principal and the financial service provider is the agent. The agent has better information about the market than the principal and the principal cannot closely supervise what the agent is up to. This provides agents with an incentive to put their own interests above those of the principal – so investors must rely on financial regulation to protect them. The principal–agent problem is an example of the issue known as 'moral hazard', which is where one party takes risks but another party suffers the consequences if things go wrong. Moral hazard occurs in many areas, not just in investment. For example, a night watchman who sleeps on the job is a moral hazard for his employer, who will bear the consequences if thieves break in. Moral hazard often occurs in situations where employees are difficult to fire, as in the public sector. In investment, misselling a product to investors and paying huge

bonuses to financial professionals out of investors' funds are typical examples of moral hazard.

Moral hazard cannot be eliminated entirely from the system, but it can
be kept within manageable limits by carefully designing the way financial
institutions are structured, developing workable rules, and establishing
effective financial regulators who have the power to punish. In the last
two decades moral hazard has greatly increased during a period of massive
global expansion of financial services and overly lax government policies,
particularly in the US, which remains the dominant player in finance. These
overly lax policies came about partly by accident, partly, it seems, through
corruption, and partly because some governments appear to have been daz-
zled by the increased tax revenue they were able to raise from the financial
services industry during the 'noughties'. It is worth pointing out that in
spite of the rhetoric about free markets during the boom years, financial
services can never really be entirely free: governments have to participate
in financial markets in many ways on many levels, and the key industry in
finance – which is banking – cannot, in the opinion of most economists, be
left to operate uncontrolled. Since the series of financial crises that began in
2007/8, many earlier warnings by 'Cassandras' about the dangers of systemic moral hazard within banking are now proving to have been correct.

Many people think that a 'Cassandra' is just a pessimistic naysayer (what
the Americans call a 'Gloomy Gus') but in ancient Greek legend Cassandra
was cursed by the gods with the gift of accurate prophecy. It was a curse
because the gods had ensured that Cassandra's true prophecies would never
be believed. Recently a naïve commentator in the *Guardian* newspaper
opined, the 'notion that the entire global financial system is riddled with
systemic fraud – and that key players in the gatekeeper roles, both in finance
and in government, including regulatory bodies, know it and choose to
quietly sustain this reality – is one that would have only recently seemed
like the frenzied hypothesis of tinhat-wearers'. Nothing could be further
from the truth, as anybody with some direct experience of financial markets
has always known. Now some of the cats are out of the bag, however, the
problems are endlessly discussed in the mainstream media that had hitherto
largely ignored them.

As the eminent *Financial Times* journalist Martin Wolf has pointed out, 'a financial sector that generates vast rewards for insiders and repeated crises for hundreds of millions of innocent bystanders is ... politically unacceptable in the long run. Those who want market-led globalisation to prosper will recognise that this is its Achilles heel'. As a private investor who does want market-led globalisation to prosper, I do indeed recognise this weakness; however, there is also the danger of overdoing the backlash and returning to the dreary Cold War era when too many restrictions on investment and finance severely limited economic prosperity in many parts of the world.

In October 2009 the Governor of the Bank of England, Mervyn King, gave a speech in which he discussed the part played by the banking industry in the financial crises, and the need for major reforms. King argued that 'banks increased both the size and leverage of their balance sheets to levels that threatened stability of the system as a whole' and then relied on governments to bail them out. This is, of course, a kind of moral hazard. If I own a bank that I know the government will not allow to fail, I have a big incentive to take wild risks, knowing the government will pay if my wild risks go wrong. According to King, 'banks and their creditors knew that if they were sufficiently important to the economy or the rest of the financial system, and things went wrong, the government would always stand behind them. And they were right.'

While government intervention may sometimes be necessary in the short term during a crisis just to keep the system from collapsing, such support cannot be sustained indefinitely. King went on to argue that there are two ways to deal with the problem: either you can create a special category of 'too big to fail' banks and regulate the hell out of them, or you can find ways of allowing banks to fail while protecting ordinary people's savings, mortgages, rates and so on.

> While government intervention may sometimes be necessary in the short term during a crisis just to keep the system from collapsing, such support cannot be sustained indefinitely.

Back in the days of stiffer regulation, prior to the 'Big Bang' of financial deregulation in the 1980s, financial services were kept strictly separate

– you could not, for instance, be a high street bank, a stock broker, a derivatives trader, a fund manager, a bond issuer, a financial adviser, a mortgage provider and an investment bank all at the same time. You can now. When deregulation first occurred, we were assured that there would be no conflicts of interest between all the different financial activities large institutions could now take on. We were told that a clever system of 'Chinese Walls' within the institutions would prevent this. This very quickly proved not to be true as illustrated by the Dennis Levine story (see Chapter 2), and the conflicts of interest within the banking system have continually grown since then.

Moral hazard within the banking system now amounts in many cases to outright fraud, but because this is institutionalised and ubiquitous it has been difficult to assign blame. When the banking scandals first began to come to light in 2007/8, it looked as if many institutions and individuals were going to get off scot-free. However, in the ensuing years, as more and more evidence of wrongdoing by banks has emerged, it has become probable that at least some of them are not going to be allowed to get away with it. To understand the scale and depth of the problems in the banking system, we'll look at two examples: the ongoing LIBOR scandal, and a severe case of corruption and 'misselling' (that's what some people might call 'cheating') in small-town USA.

The LIBOR scandal

The London Interbank Offered Rate (LIBOR) is a collection of interest rates for major currencies and time periods that are used as reference rates for a wide range of financial transactions. LIBOR rates are calculated every morning of every banking day, and are based on an average of the rates a range of banks, known as 'panel banks' say they would have to pay if they borrowed from another bank on that day in a specific currency for a specific (short-term) time period. The data are submitted at 11.10 a.m. and then published by Thomson Reuters at 11.30 a.m. each day. In order to prevent manipulation, the upper and lower quartiles of the data submitted by panel banks are ignored, and the rate is based on the middle two quartiles of the data. LIBOR rates are very important benchmarks for transactions around the world, especially for derivatives deals (at least $350 trillion in derivatives are linked to LIBOR) that are sensitive to small changes in the rate. LIBOR was set up in the 1980s to ensure that rates on corporate lending did not fall below the rates at which banks were lending to each other.

In June 2012 the UK's Financial Services Authority (FSA) fined Barclays Bank £59.5 million for acting 'inappropriately' on occasion between 2005 and 2008 by allowing its submission to Thomson Reuters to be influenced by the demands of its own derivatives traders, and traders at other banks. The FSA also found that Barclays had tried to influence the submissions of other banks relating to US dollar LIBOR and EURIBOR (a similar benchmark based on euros), and had also made 'inappropriate LIBOR submissions to avoid negative media comment' between 2007 and 2009 during the banking crisis. In its notice to Barclays about the fine, the FSA quotes extensively from emails and conversations between traders and those responsible for submitting the rates each day that demonstrate a conscious desire to manipulate the rates. For example, 'on 8 October 2008, a Submitter was asked about Barclays' LIBOR submissions during a telephone conversation. He responded that "[Manager E]*'s asked me to put it lower than it was yesterday ... to send the message that we're not in the shit"*.'

In the same month, Barclays was fined $160 million by the US Justice Department and $200 million by the US Commodities Futures Trading Commission in relation to this 'inappropriate' behaviour, which the American agencies, in contrast to the mealy-mouthed FSA, robustly termed 'manipulation'. The bank's Chairman, Philip Agius, and CEO, Bob Diamond, both promptly resigned. It has been open season on banks since the financial crisis began in 2007/8, and the media around the world have had a field day.

> It has been open season on banks since the financial crisis began in 2007/8, and the media around the world have had a field day.

At the time of writing, at least ten more regulators round the world are looking into possible wrongdoing by the panel banks that help set

LIBOR. It had already been plain that Barclays had not been the only bank up to no good, and it did not come as an enormous surprise in December 2012 when the Swiss bank UBS was fined $1.2 billion by the US Justice Department and the Commodities Futures Trading Commission, 60 million Swiss francs by the Swiss regulators and £160 million by the FSA for its role in the affair. UBS had been caught with more than 2,000 documented instances of its employees conspiring to manipulate LIBOR rates between 2005 and 2010 with a recklessness and arrogance that beggars belief. They knew that their phone conversations were recorded and their emails were kept, but in many cases they openly discussed their wrongdoing. Even the Mafia talk in code! It also emerged that not only banks, but interbroker dealers (who are intermediaries between banks) were also involved.

In 2013, the Royal Bank of Scotland was fined £390 million and it is very likely that many other banks will follow. In the US, a torrent of lawsuits has been unleashed by corporations and municipalities who claim to have been forced to overpay on their borrowings because of the manipulation of LIBOR rates. Regulators around the world seem at last to be prepared to act in concert to curb the arrogant cynicism of the banks. Better still, it appears that regulators may move against banks for the widespread misselling of interest rate swaps (see Jefferson County below).

Well, let's not get too excited. By the time you read this, the LIBOR affair may be ancient history. Some bankers may even have been sent to prison, but banks will still be here. We can't function without them. And no amount of regulation will prevent them from acting, in the FSA's immortal understatement, 'inappropriately' if the opportunity appears.

The swindling of Jefferson County, Alabama

In 1996, following lawsuits by the US Environmental Protection Agency and others, a court ordered Jefferson County, the most heavily populated county in Alabama, to renovate and expand its sewer system to prevent sewage overflows into a number of rivers. The County duly began to raise

money for this purpose, and between 1997 and late 2002 it issued a succession of warrants (a type of bond) paying fixed rates of interest. Although
critics complained that the project was unnecessarily ambitious, original
estimates of the cost of the sewer project were around $250 million, a tiny
fraction of the debt that Jefferson County eventually incurred. As with most
public projects, costs began to escalate as suppliers sought to pump up
their share of this lucrative scheme. Charles LeCroy, then at the financial
services firm Raymond James, arranged most of the fixed-interest warrants.
Then, in 2002, LeCroy went to work for the regional office of JPMorgan
Chase, the investment bank, and brought a lot of his municipal customers
with him.

LeCroy set up a deal with William Blount, a local business consultant,
to persuade Jefferson County to refinance their borrowings for the sewage
project. Between late 2002 and late 2003, Jefferson County issued three
new bond offerings at variable rates of interest, raising approximately
$3 billion – considerably more than the original estimate of $250 million for the sewage scheme – which were arranged and underwritten
by JPMorgan Chase. These arrangements had the effect of changing the
County's bond debts from sensible and predictable fixed interest rates to
not very sensible and considerably riskier variable interest rates. The variable rate offered the dubious benefit of lower interest payments in the
short term, together with the likelihood that they would rise substantially
in the future. They also generated millions of dollars in fees, not only for
JPMorgan and William Blount's firm, Blount Parrish, but also for a range
of other local outfits associated with County commissioners.

Worse was to come: during the same period Jefferson County also
entered into a number of interest rate swap agreements with a total
notional value of $5.6 billion, mostly with JPMorgan. An interest rate
swap is a derivative contract where two parties agree to swap interest payments on specific sums for an agreed time period. The purpose of the
interest rate swaps was supposed to be to 'fix' the interest payments the
County would be making on the variable rate bonds it had just issued.
Like the refinanced bonds, the interest rate swaps also generated large fees
for JPMorgan and Blount Parrish, and, according to the prosecution in

a court case against JPMorgan and others, 'the price the county paid for these transactions in terms of fees and interest rates was artificially inflated by millions of dollars, to account in part for the fact that JPMorgan's scheme to secure the county's business included bribes, kickbacks and pay-offs the Defendants paid to or received from each other.' It is estimated that Jefferson County was overcharged by as much as $100 million on the swaps.

According to the complaint in another court case brought by the SEC in 2009 against LeCroy and Douglas McFaddin, another JPMorgan executive, early in 2002, LeCroy had corresponded with his superiors at JPMorgan to propose that the bank pay bribes to two small local stock broking firms to get them to influence Jefferson County commissioners to give the sewer bond business to JPMorgan. LeCroy suggested that such payments would be modest – $5,000 to $25,000 per deal – and received a positive response from one of his bosses. According to the SEC, as the sales drive progressed many payments were made to more local people, totalling millions of dollars. In mid-2002 LeCroy and McFaddin targeted two County commissioners who had lost their elections and were due to leave office in November, and who wished to see the two small local stockbroking firms receive their backhanders from JPMorgan. A taped conversation between LeCroy and McFaddin was presented as evidence, showing that the two executives had discussed how to redraft an invoice from one of the stockbrokers to 'conceal the firm's lack of participation in the transaction'.

In November 2002 Larry Langford, a long-time friend of William Blount, became head of the Jefferson County Commission. Blount urged Langford to do a swap with Goldman Sachs, not JPMorgan, because his firm had a consulting arrangement with Goldman. Blount arranged loans and cash payments for Langford and bought him expensive designer clothing as an inducement to keep Blount Parrish involved in the bond and swap deals. LeCroy and McFaddin negotiated with Langford to pay Goldman millions to stay out of the deals – and Blount Parrish received $2.5 million from JPMorgan's profits. These payments were disguised; in the case of the Goldman pay-off, JPMorgan created a fictitious swap contract to transfer the money. From then on, every time the County did a bond or swap deal with JPMorgan, Langford and Blount received hefty payments, as well as other commissioners and associates, and a few Wall Street firms.

The litany of the bribes paid goes on and on. It makes appalling reading, but it should not distract us from the even more outrageous fact that Jefferson County wound up borrowing $3 billion through issuing bonds, and had been persuaded to enter into very risky interest rate swaps that it did not need. Through the petty greed of local officials and businesspeople, and the ruthlessness of JPMorgan, the County had made itself hostage to massive liabilities that would eventually go very wrong indeed.

In the meantime, however, there was trouble brewing in the construction end of the sewer project. A 2003 engineering report found that there was massive waste and little coordination of the programme, and estimated that there was up to $100 million in 'accounting discrepancies' between relevant County departments. In 2005 the FBI indicted 21 County officials, commissioners and contractors, the majority of whom have been convicted of bribery and received large fines and short prison terms. In 2006, the SEC began to investigate the County's bond and swap deals.

Then, in 2007, came the US housing crash. Early in 2008 the County's insurers had their ratings downgraded, forcing up interest payments, and the County's own credit status was downgraded to junk by Standard & Poor's. These events triggered penalties in its swap deals, so now it had to pay off in excess of $800 million in four years, rather than the forty years originally agreed. Underwriting banks were forced to take up unsold bonds, for which they imposed large penalties. In 2009, the cost of servicing Jefferson County's debts had risen to $636 million, from $53 million in the previous year. There was also a problem with the interest rate swaps themselves; JPMorgan was paying the County a low rate based on LIBOR, while the County had to pay its bondholders a much higher rate. Jefferson County began to default on its interest payments.

In 2009 Larry Langford, who had risen to become Mayor in 2007, was convicted of receiving bribes worth more than $200,000 in relation to the sewer financing and was eventually sentenced to 15 years in prison. Blount,

> Water rates have shot through the roof, courthouses are being closed down and schools starved of essential funds – and all because some bent local politicians were outwitted by the outrageous predatory practices of Wall Street firms.

the fixer, received fines and a sentence of more than four years. JPMorgan paid the SEC a fine of $25 million, returned $50 million to Jefferson County, and was forced to abandon its demand for $647 million in termination fees from the County. LeCroy, who had been fired by JPMorgan in 2004 over an unrelated matter, is still being pursued in court by the SEC at the time of writing.

For Jefferson County, all this retribution has been too little, too late. In 2011 it declared bankruptcy. Water rates have shot through the roof, courthouses are being closed down and schools starved of essential funds – and all because some bent local politicians were outwitted by the outrageous predatory practices of Wall Street firms.

Surviving the banks

Top bankers are powerful and often have a great deal of influence on politicians, which may be one reason why so few senior bankers have gone to jail, and why efforts to reform the banking system have been so slow to have any effect. There have clearly been many rearguard actions by the banks to defend themselves against attempts to make them change the way they operate. For example, in the UK there have been repeated threats by major banks to leave the country if reforms are too harsh. In the eurozone, continental banks lent heavily to the wrong people (for example the Greek government) in the belief that the political will to make the Eurozone work would ensure the banks would be bailed out if the loans went bad. They may yet be proved right, as European politicians appear unwilling to face up to the economic chaos that they have helped to create by pursuing a grandiose ideology of EU integration while ignoring economic realities. In the US there are signs of a new determination to deal more harshly with the excesses of predatory financial institutions. The case for breaking up the large banks and separating the utilitarian banking functions, such as high street banking, completely from riskier activities such as investment banking seems very strong, as it would help to protect the real economy from the excesses bankers have committed in the financial markets. But such a profound restructuring of the industry would require a concerted effort by governments around the world and very widespread political support. In spite of enormous public outrage at bankers' behaviour during the 'noughties', there has not yet been any strong move to break the grotesque bonus culture in the sector, which has plainly increased moral hazard and cannot be justified on the grounds of attracting talent. Excessive bonuses have incentivised finance professionals not only to take excessive risks but also to flout the rules that were designed to keep the system stable; if this is allowed to continue, we can expect to see another large crisis in the sector within a decade or two.

9

Due negligence: failing to do the analysis

Of course, no one wants to take undue career risk by sticking their head up and saying the emperor isn't wearing any clothes but ...

Harry Markopolos, Madoff's whistleblower

These days investors are swamped with information about markets, industries and companies. Even if you spent your whole life ploughing through the material, you could never master it all. Realising this, many investors simply give up, and make arbitrary, often inconsistent, investment decisions or rely on the assurances of the organisations involved in selling them investments. But how can an investor happily accept statements made by any financial services company at face value in a time when we know that so many of them are incentivised to put their own interests above those of their customers? Investors really do need to make an effort to perform as much due diligence as possible; in essence, due diligence means independently verifying all the key elements of the investment on offer, and considering all the possible risks.

Let's see how a private investor's due diligence can work in practice. I have been looking at the services offered by a firm that provides an online portfolio management service (let's call it 'Firm X'). The investments are restricted to Exchange Traded Funds (ETFs), which are a relatively new kind of collective investment that are marketed as a transparent, straight-forward investment vehicle with low management charges, and are growing in popularity. I knew something about ETFs, but had never put any time into trying to understand what they really are and how they really work. Now that Firm X had caught my attention – mainly through its emphasis on the ease of use, low charges, and the facility to monitor your invest-ments closely – I felt I had to learn more. And that's where due diligence begins: first of all, you do really need to understand the investment you are being offered. Firm X's website is helpful and informative, but it definitely does not tell you everything you need to know. Although its initial adver-tising (which I noticed on the London Underground) didn't say so, Firm X's website explained, not very prominently, that it only offers a discretion-ary service, which means you tell them roughly what your investment aims are and they decide what ETFs to buy and sell on your behalf. There is nothing wrong necessarily with a discretionary service, but it does take away some decision-making power from the investor, so that feature immediately went down in my notebook as something to think about further. I also felt slightly uncomfortable that it seemed quite possible for an ordinary person (the ad on the London Underground depicted a girl in her twenties happily managing her portfolio on her laptop) to invest without really understand-ing all the implications and risks. This is not to suggest Firm X is anything other than a respectable firm, but it alerted me to the fact that the sales pitch was a bit too consumer-orientated for my taste; yes, I want things to be easy, but I don't want to be patronised.

Then I started to read up on ETFs. I quickly discovered that they are controversial. An article in the *Financial Times* quoted a fund manager who is 'a fierce critic of ETFs' as saying, 'there is a certainty that ETFs are being missold to the retail market and that the risks being incurred in running, constructing, trading and holding them are not sufficiently understood.' A fact sheet from the FSA talks about the risks of Exchange Traded Products (ETPs) and explains, although most ETPs are funds (i.e. ETFs), some are structured as debt securities – so that point goes down in my notebook as something to check, since I had already noticed Firm X's website mentioned investing in commodities, which the FSA gives as an example of a debt security ETP. Then I notice that Kweku Adoboli, a UBS trader who lost the bank $2.3 billion in unauthorised trading and was convicted of fraud in 2012, had been trading ETFs – definitely another point on my list of things to investigate further. I start reading endless articles debating whether or not ETFs and ETPs are a good thing. I noted that HSBC 'only offers physical ETFs on the basis that individual investors have a better chance of understanding them', and there are also 'synthetic ETFs', which invest in 'bespoke derivatives, or swaps, to deliver the performance of the relevant index or stockmarket.' I am pretty sure I don't want my money going into synthetic ETFs, so that's one more thing to check with Firm X.

After a few hours' reading, I have had enough, and decide to exercise the one fantastic right that private investors have and so many finance professionals don't: I decide to defer my decision. Maybe I'll come back to it later, and maybe I won't; I don't have anyone breathing down my neck asking why I haven't done anything, the way finance professionals do, and I don't have to justify my decision to anyone. I have decided not to decide, and I feel great!

From what I have learned so far, ETFs are a lot more complicated than they first appeared, and I particularly don't like the fact that some index-tracking ETFs track an index that has been custom-made for that ETF – as the FSA points out, 'if the institution that creates the index is affiliated to the ETP provider, it may have an incentive to select the individual constituents of the index to optimise its own revenues, rather than that of the investor'. This particular FSA document is intended for investment advisers and contains a lot of juicy technical questions on a wide range of risk issues. These questions can go on my due diligence list should I ever decide to investigate further.

> I have decided not to decide, and I feel great!

Most of the due diligence that you do should result in a 'no' or 'do nothing' decision fairly early in the process, so it is less work than it may appear at first. You only have to turn into a terrier burrowing for rabbits if what you are finding looks good and you want to invest. Yes, this kind of due diligence takes some time and effort, but you haven't had to pay for any fancy lawyers or analysts to do the work for you, so the cost is low. If you are the kind of person who can't or won't do this kind of analysis you probably won't be reading this book anyway, but if you are analytically inclined, you might reasonably complain that it is all too much work, and you would much rather find someone you trust to do all the heavy lifting for you. And that was what Bernie Madoff offered.

As the process described above has illustrated, there are clearly many limitations to the amount of due diligence that a private investor can do. Unless you happen to be a very specialised investment lawyer, for example, you probably won't have the skills to understand all the legal issues involved. And unless you knew a lot about options, you probably could not have understood completely the 'split-strike conversion strategy' that Madoff falsely claimed to be using to generate his steady returns, but the beauty of a healthy and vigorous financial press is there are people out there writing articles who know more than you do on particular investment issues. There are also a lot of people out there writing articles who know considerably less than you do, but with practice you can learn to weed them out.

The Madoff scandal was a huge surprise when it emerged in 2008, but as we saw earlier (Chapter 3) there had been two sceptical articles about Madoff in the financial press in 2001, one in the *MARHedge* trade journal entitled 'Madoff tops charts; skeptics ask how', and the other in the better-known *Barron's* magazine entitled 'Don't Ask, Don't Tell'. You might not have found the *MARHedge* article by browsing the internet in 2001, but you certainly would have found the *Barron's* article. Incidentally, private investors should try to punch above their weight in their choice of investment reading matter – even if you don't understand everything, it is a good idea to read professional and academic investment articles, and not to confine yourself only to the mainstream media, which tends to dumb things down.

So, let's consider what a private investor could have gleaned about Madoff's operation from the two 2001 articles. 'Don't Ask, Don't Tell' informs us that Madoff is well-known on Wall Street as a top market maker for the NASDAQ stock market, is very active on the New York Stock Exchange, but also it is less well known, he manages more than $6 billion of rich people's money. So far, so good, but then there is this: 'What's more, these private accounts have produced compound average annual returns of 15% for more than a decade. Remarkably, some of the larger, billion-dollar Madoff-run funds have never had a down year.'

Never had a down year? Returns of 15% a year for more than a decade? At the very least, we need to know how he did it. The article gives us a potted description of how Madoff's split-strike conversion strategy is supposed to work, and then tells us that there is speculation Madoff's market-making arm subsidises his investment funds to 'smooth' the investment returns. If true, this would definitely not be OK, but the article reports Madoff's firm denial that he does this, and then goes on to quote a number of people who don't believe it is possible to achieve such good returns from a split-strike conversion strategy. Madoff naturally says they are wrong. It then goes on to discuss Madoff's secrecy, citing an investment manager who withdrew money from Madoff, saying, 'when he couldn't explain how they were up or down in a particular month ... I pulled the money out'. So, we can't find out how he does it. That alone deserves a big bold point on your due diligence list. It might not have been enough to stop you investing, but it certainly should have been enough to prevent you from putting all your life savings into Madoff, as some of his victims are alleged to have done.

Let's suppose that you also obtained the *MARHedge* article. It's longer and more technical, but the central message is perfectly clear: many investment professionals cannot understand how Madoff has achieved good, steady returns for 11 years using a split-strike conversion strategy, because normally you would expect more volatility (ups and downs) in the returns. Note that neither article even whispers the word 'fraud' – in general, the responsible end of the financial press will never cry 'fraud' until someone has been arrested. Nevertheless, the *MARHedge* article identified the key due diligence issue, namely that no one could figure out how Bernie did it. That would have been enough for me to walk away; personally, I never want to invest in a mystery, even if it means I might lose out on some

juicy profits. It reminds me too much of the company that invited investment 'for carrying on an *undertaking of great advantage but no one to know
what it is*' during the South Sea Bubble of 1720 (the promoter of that one
absconded with all the money).

Harry Markopolos and Bernie Madoff

Harry Markopolos is an unprepossessing, nerdy fellow who also happens to
be a maths whizz and a Chartered Financial Analyst. In a 2005 letter to the
SEC he described himself as a derivatives expert with 'experience managing split-strike conversion products both using index options and individual
stock options both with and without index puts. Very few people in the
world have the mathematical background needed to manage these types of
products but I am one of them'.

As mentioned earlier (Chapter 3), Markopolos repeatedly approached
the SEC between 2000 and 2008 with plausible evidence that there was
something wrong with Madoff's investment operation. At the time he
began this crusade, Markopolos was working at a small options trading
firm in Boston. His firm was a competitor to Madoff in a small way, and
Markopolos was asked by his boss in 1999 to see if he could construct a
split-strike conversion strategy similar to the one Madoff was supposed to
be using, with a view to attracting some custom for his own firm. In a TV
interview Markopolos gave in 2011, he claimed that when he first examined
some Madoff data, 'in five minutes I knew, I said this is totally bogus'. The
document he had examined was a one-page marketing aid from the Broyhill
All-Weather Fund (one of the feeder funds that invested in Madoff) that
described Madoff's investment strategy and stated the monthly returns
between 1993 and March 2000.

So let's see the kinds of things that an expert (Markopolos) was able
to figure out by studying Madoff's operation from the outside in a few
hours of initial analysis. Markopolos says that he suspected fraud so quickly
because the strategy, as described in the Broyhill document 'would have
had trouble beating a 0% return.' He knew this, he says, because he had

been managing a 'slightly similar' options strategy and knew from experience that it was not possible to have as few loss-making months as Madoff's figures suggested. He then entered the Broyhill monthly figures in a spreadsheet, noticing that Madoff seemed to be confused about which stock market index he was using as a benchmark, the S&P 500 or the S&P 100 (these two indices perform very differently from one another). Markopolos found that Madoff's performance had a very low correlation (6%) with the S&P 500 and, more importantly, while Madoff had had only 3 down months out of a total of 87 months, the S&P 500 had been down in 28 months during the same period.

Markopolos then obtained statistical data from the Chicago Board of Trade concerning the number of options being traded for the S&P 100, the index that Madoff's strategy was explicitly supposed to be replicating (despite Madoff's constant references to the S&P 500). He found that there were not enough index options in existence for Madoff to have been able to have run his options strategy as described in the Broyhill data. There appeared to be two possible explanations of what was going on. The first was that Madoff was illegally 'front-running', which is when a broker has a stream of large orders to execute in the market, and profits from this information by trading on his own account minutes in advance of executing his clients' orders. Performing further mathematical modelling, Markopolos found that front-running Madoff's portfolio of billions of dollars could indeed have generated extra returns that might account for his stellar performance, assuming he put these illegal profits back into his clients' funds. Markopolos thought in 2000 and 2001 that this was the most likely explanation, but as Madoff's funds under management grew in subsequent years, it became evident that front-running could no longer explain Madoff's continued steady returns. Nevertheless, as we saw earlier (Chapter 3), SEC investigations continued to work on the front-running hypothesis for several years afterwards.

The second possible explanation for Madoff's returns – which eventually turned out to be correct – was that Madoff wasn't actually investing at all, and instead was simply making up his monthly returns as part of a massive Ponzi scheme.

So why hadn't anyone else noticed this problem, given that many large financial institutions had put customers' money into Madoff in one way or another? In his 2011 TV interview Markopolos argues that these institutions, particularly those in Europe, did think that Madoff was a crook, but they thought he was stealing from clients using his broker–dealer arm to subsidise his funds. According to Markopolos, the institutions did not ask Madoff the questions they could and should have asked because they would have then been implicated if they had continued to send clients to Madoff after discovering any wrongdoing. Why did they want to go on putting clients on to Madoff? Because Madoff paid unusually high fees to institutions that brought him business, says Markopolos, and they didn't want to lose these fees.

A word on funds and funds of funds

Many of Madoff's victims who invested through feeder funds, we are told, were unaware that their money had ended up being managed by Madoff. This suggests that there was quite a problem of lack of transparency in these funds, which in itself would be a definite black mark in a due diligence exercise. But another problem with feeder funds and funds of funds (the latter are funds that only invest in other funds) is that they add an extra layer of charges, which in many cases offsets any gains you might have made by investing in them, and, indeed, may substantially reduce your overall return. As we saw earlier (Chapter 6), there is good reason to doubt that fund managers actually bring anything of value to the table, since the majority of them do not outperform the indices used as benchmarks to judge performance. It follows, therefore, that you are likely to obtain a better return in the long term by investing in a true index fund (unfortunately there are now many index funds that do not truly mimic an index) with low, low charges.

Terry Smith is a British analyst who in 1990 published the excellent *Accounting for Growth*, which exposed the deceitful accounting practices being used by many rapidly growing companies at that time. More recently

Smith made an interesting analysis of what would have happened to investors in Warren Buffet's company, Berkshire Hathaway, if he had run it as
a fund with typical hedge fund charges, instead of it being a company in
which you and he are fellow shareholders who share the profits. As is well
known, Buffett's long-term performance has been very good, even though
it has slowed in recent years, as Buffett predicted, because Berkshire is so
big now it is harder to find investments that really make a difference to the
annual return. Between 1965 and 2009 a $1,000 initial investment with
Buffett would have grown into $4.8 million by the end of the period in
nominal terms (to find out what $4.8 million would be in 1965 dollars,
you would have to adjust for inflation, but it would still be an excellent
return). Smith argues that if 'Buffett had set it up as a hedge fund and
charged 2 per cent of the value of the funds as an annual fee plus 20 per
cent of any gains, of that $4.8m, $4.4m would belong to him as manager
and only $400,000 would belong to you, the investor. And this is the result
you would get if your hedge fund manager had equalled Warren Buffett's
performance. Believe me, he or she won't.'

For investors, any charges are a bad thing, because they reduce your
return. Sometimes they may be unavoidable – you can't for instance buy
and sell shares for free – but fund charges are absolutely avoidable. To avoid
them, all you have to do is not invest in the fund! If you invest in an index
tracker fund, you will pay charges, but the total expense ratio (TER), which
measures the total costs to investors including all fees, can be as low as 0.27%.
That's just over a quarter of 1%, which most people can live with. Yes, index
trackers won't beat the index, and some hot-shot managers do beat the index
for a while, but only very few, like the glorious Warren Buffett, have been
able to do it spectacularly over many decades. Sadly, it is probably too late
to obtain spectacular returns by investing in Berkshire because of its size,
and when Buffett finally retires or passes away, it is highly unlikely that any
replacement will be able to match his long-term performance.

So here's another point about due diligence; remember that you, the
investor, are investing for your whole life. Funds and fund managers come
and go, and there is a clear moral hazard if they are getting rewarded by
short-term performance and taking a cut out of your assets every year.

Due diligence always matters

Glib assurances are no substitute for doing your own due diligence as much as possible. If you buy a house, for instance, you would take a lot of trouble to find out everything you could about it yourself, as well as paying experts – lawyers and surveyors – to make further checks that you cannot do properly yourself. Although some people unwisely try to cut corners by, for instance, not paying for a full structural survey, most people understand this is a false economy. Sensible people will also bring along a builder they trust to view the house, to help them understand what any renovations or additions are likely to entail. They will walk around the neighbourhood and talk to local people about it. They will visit the house at different times of the day to get a feeling for

> **Many of these fussy house buyers are much less fussy about choosing financial investments, which makes no sense at all.**

things like traffic and noise levels. They will compare prices and research planning issues. In short, people tend to be very, very fussy about buying a house, not only because they don't want to be sold a pup but also because they really want to understand what they are letting themselves in for. That's due diligence! Many of these fussy house buyers are much less fussy about choosing financial investments, which makes no sense at all.

Doing due diligence is not just about spotting possible fraud; it is also about making sure that you properly understand what you are investing in. Some kinds of ETFs, for instance, may be right for you, but if you don't understand how ETFs work, you are leaving yourself open to potentially nasty surprises, quite unnecessarily. So make sure that you really do understand what you are buying. And, to continue the house-buying analogy, you wouldn't buy a house just because a lawyer or a surveyor told you to, would you? So why would you invest in something just because a financial adviser or a salesperson told you to do so? Now, there are some very wise old advisers and brokers who know what they are talking about, but most of the ones you will encounter are just reasonably well-trained drones. They will follow the regulations and conduct a 'fact find' into your circumstances and risk appetite before recommending investments, but those investments may be considerably less bespoke than they seem – and cases of misselling occur with monotonous regularity. So don't switch off your brain just because you have an adviser!

PART FOUR

How to avoid being swindled

10

Funds are not all the same!

I'm a proven liar. Don't believe anything I say.

Sam Israel III, founder of the Bayou Group

In the UK, unit trusts and investment trusts have a very good safety record in terms of fraud; for example, according to the Association of Unit Trusts and Investment Funds, no investor has ever lost money in a UK unit trust as a result of fraud. Tough regulations – along with a determination in the industry not to kill the golden goose – have been very effective for a long period. Unit trusts are especially tightly controlled, with limitations on how much they can invest in unlisted stocks, how few investments they can own, and are usually prohibited from borrowing money or going 'short' in the market. As well as making it more difficult to commit fraud, these measures are designed to limit the potential for a sudden, nasty loss in a market downturn.

Such fraud as does occur has been perpetrated by third parties, in particular by fraudulent sales organisations called 'boiler rooms', operating out of an office in another country with lax financial regulation. Once a boiler room sales force has found a live prospect, they can be very persuasive, and every year hundreds of investors part with substantial sums for shares that turn out to be worthless. Sometimes a boiler room will claim, fraudulently, to be selling a fund registered in the UK, without the knowledge or involvement of that fund, but more often the fund offered will have a

> It is a little difficult to be sympathetic towards the victims of boiler room fraud. It is so avoidable.

similar name to a UK fund and be registered overseas. It is a little difficult to be sympathetic towards the victims of boiler room fraud. It is so avoidable.

I am contacted by boiler room salespeople several times a year, and have listened patiently to the sales pitch, which often continues in many telephone calls over a period of weeks. The salespeople are energetic and eager to persuade, but there are obvious problems with the deals they offer. They make optimistic claims about the potential rewards that are plainly in breach of FSA regulations. They pretend that their deals have hitherto only been available to top investors, and this is a unique chance to get in on the deal. They have elaborate and implausible stories about why they are not currently registered in the UK. They are reluctant to give verifiable information. Their explanations of why their investments are going to succeed insult the intelligence. And, most important of all, they cold-called you (a fact that they will try to make you forget). No legitimate professional will call you offering an investment product unless you have invited them to do so – so if you receive an unsolicited call, just put the phone down.

Apart from boiler room fraud, which is not the fund industry's fault, investors can be confident that the chance of outright fraud when investing in UK-registered funds is very low. This does not necessarily make such funds good investments. Overwhelmingly, the evidence of many studies shows that the majority of funds do not consistently outperform the stock market indices against which they should be measured; this contradicts the basic premise of a fund, which is the fund manager is better than you are at choosing investments, and can outperform the market. The statistical evidence is that the majority of fund managers do not do this consistently over the long term. As this knowledge has become more widely understood, there has been a rise in investment in 'index tracker' funds, which mechanically mimic the performance of a chosen index, such as the FTSE 100, at very low cost. Tracker funds are attractive to investors who are frustrated with the performance of their fund investments, but do not want to micromanage their investments themselves.

In recent years a new type of fund has become very prominent: the hedge fund. Unlike most traditional funds, hedge funds are almost completely free of restrictions on the investments they make, and are thus able to take on much higher risks. All other things being equal, higher risk is associated with higher returns, so one would expect a high-risk hedge fund that is successful to generate high returns. However, higher risk is also associated with higher losses, so one would expect a high-risk hedge fund that was not successful to suffer unusually heavy losses. Another way of saying this is that taking on more risk leads to more volatility and the returns from high-risk hedge funds will tend to be more volatile (i.e. they will tend to hit bigger highs and lows than a lower-risk strategy).

The first hedge fund is thought to have been one established by a *Fortune* magazine journalist, Alfred Winslow Jones, in 1949. Jones raised $100,000 to run an investment partnership that tried to make profits by hedging (in this case, buying stocks he expected to rise, and selling short stocks that he expected to fall). Like most hedge funds today, Jones's fund asked for a performance fee of 20% from the profits, and placed restrictions on withdrawals (including lock-up periods and requiring notice for withdrawals). It is often objected that the managers of a hedge fund are sharing in any profits but not bearing any share of the potential losses; this issue is mitigated to some extent by the fact that hedge fund managers generally have substantial sums of their own money invested in their hedge funds, thereby further incentivising good performance. Another feature of Jones's fund that also applies to hedge funds today is it was designed to appeal to well-heeled and sophisticated investors who were in a position to appreciate the risks; investors were approached privately, without advertising to the public, thereby avoiding most regulatory requirements.

Jones's fund performed well. Between 1949 and 1968 it produced a total return of 500%, stimulating the interest of wealthy individuals, many of whom held senior positions in the financial industry. During the 1960s a number of other hedge funds appeared – including a very successful one run by famed investors George Soros and Jim Rogers – but many of them did not use the 'hedging' strategy used by Alfred Winslow Jones, and pursued a variety of objectives with the aid of high borrowing (thus increasing potential risks and returns). Hedge funds virtually disappeared in the 1970s during adverse market conditions, but revived during the deregulation of the 1980s, when George Soros set up his Quantum Fund that famously helped force the UK out of the EU's Exchange Rate Mechanism. In their 1980s and 1990s incarnation, hedge funds – which only numbered about 150 – were seen as quite useful for the world's markets because they would pounce on any market inefficiency, such as those caused by government policy, and exploit it until it had disappeared. They were seen as the preserve of market insiders who knew what they were doing, and since they were not seeking money from the general public, the fact that they were not at all transparent and were subject to little regulation was not thought to be a serious problem.

Then, in the 1990s, a very large hedge fund, Long Term Capital Management (LTCM), was set up to exploit new investment formulae devised by Nobel Prize-winning economists. The techniques involved taking long and short positions in a range of different markets and asset types, including the extensive use of derivatives. The bulk of LTCM's activity, however, was in government bonds around the world, and its main bet was essentially that interest rates in different countries would tend to converge. Between 1994 and 1998 LTCM produced annual returns of more than 40%. In 1998 it was caught out by the Russian government's default on its bonds, losing an estimated $6 billion. More losses followed, and it soon emerged that LTCM's leverage – it had a $1 trillion exposure on its positions – was so large that it threatened the global financial system. US banks, at the behest of the government, stepped in to bail out LTCM and limit its losses while it gradually unwound its complex positions. Although there was criticism at the time from fanatical advocates of the free market (along the lines that in a free market, failing organisations should be left to fail), the risk that LTCM's collapse would set off a very serious crisis was very real, and the US authorities were probably right to act as they did.

Thus, by the 1990s the large size, aggressive style, high risk-taking, and appetite for massive debt in the major hedge funds were a cause for concern, especially as many of them were using derivatives so intensively that it was impossible to assess the potential risks to market stability. Then, driven by customer demand, the hedge fund industry changed direction and began to move away from the handful of super-rich, financially sophisticated investors down towards the mass market. Between 2000 and 2011 there was an explosion in the number of hedge funds (from around 4,000 worldwide to nearly 10,000) and in the amount of money they managed (from $1 billion to nearly $2 billion, down from its peak of $2.5 billion in 2007). While not exactly reaching the most vulnerable of investors, the proliferation of hedge funds has made them available to a much wider range of investors who, while they may have been affluent, were not necessarily sufficiently financially sophisticated to understand exactly what they were doing. The new generation of hedge funds also attracted institutional investors, including investments by other funds.

From the point of view of an investment manager, starting a hedge fund is currently rather attractive. As the manager of such a fund, you can take 20% of any profits you make, and, unlike Jones's original fund, most hedge funds also make a management charge of up to 2%. By locking in investors for a period – often a year – and then only allowing withdrawals at fixed dates, you have far more control than, say, unit trusts do over how much money you have to invest, because you are not as vulnerable to a sudden rush of investor withdrawals. Free from the restrictions imposed on other types of fund, you can plunge in and out of any type of investment that you want, anywhere in the world, whether or not they are quoted on any market. As someone confident in your own abilities, you will of course have no objection to adding to the fund part of that large pile of cash you earned in bonuses while you were learning your trade.

It is perhaps too early to tell if all this freedom will lead to problems in the hedge fund industry as it is presently constituted. Hedge funds can choose from an extremely wide range of investment strategies. Popular strategies include hedging in equities, the 'macro' approach (taking large positions in different markets in anticipation of a major event), special situations, such as mergers, and 'relative value' methods, which involve trying to identify mispriced financial instruments using complex formulae. Some funds use multiple strategies, and recently 'funds of funds' have emerged that specialise in investing solely in other hedge funds – while this latter type of fund might be attractive to the smaller investor who cannot afford the large investment required to invest directly in a specific hedge fund, it is very difficult to see how a fund of funds can offer value for money, given the additional layer of management charges.

A study by the Financial Services Authority (FSA), the main UK regulator, recognises the systemic dangers presented by hedge funds but suggests that these are not as severe as has been feared. In the UK, hedge fund managers are subject to some regulation by the FSA, but the hedge funds they manage are not regulated significantly, except for a prohibition on marketing them to the public. In the US, hedge funds are similarly lightly regulated, and the smaller ones may not be required to register with the SEC or to provide it with any public reports. Although, like any business, it is illegal for hedge funds to commit fraud, the lack of transparency in the operations of individual hedge funds provides an opening for fraudsters, and the lack of investor protection makes this all the more dangerous for investors. There have been a number of frauds involving hedge funds, but they do not appear to form a pattern in terms of the type of fraud committed. The lack of transparency allows a wide range of frauds to be attempted.

> **The lack of transparency allows a wide range of frauds to be attempted.**

These include: the manager of Lion Capital Management, a San Francisco hedge fund, who stole more than $500,000 from a retired teacher who thought the money was going into the fund; an investment manager who controlled a number of hedge funds through which he operated a $37 million Ponzi scheme; and a number of cases in which managers exaggerated the value of certain assets (usually of assets not listed on any market) to hide trading losses from their investors.

The Bayou hedge fund fraud

With the exception of Bernie Madoff, to date, the largest hedge fund fraud has been that of the Bayou Group, which collapsed in 2006 owing its investors some $300 million. The group's founder, Sam Israel, was the scion of a well-known family of commodity traders, but had started out at the bottom in Wall Street before establishing his own hedge fund in 1996 in order to trade using his proprietary computer program, 'Forward Propagation', that was supposed to provide accurate short-term 'buy' signals.

The year 1996 was the beginning of a bull run in the stock market, but Bayou, with a small fund of less than $1 million, lost 14%. When the time came for the audit, Israel and his company accountant Dan Marino knew they were in trouble; if Bayou's first year showed a loss, it would probably have to close down. Marino had an idea. The Bayou Group consisted of the hedge fund itself and a broker–dealer to execute transactions on behalf of the fund. What if the broker–dealer simply rebated all its commissions to the hedge fund? The total of the commissions was more than double the fund's losses. Grant Thornton, the independent auditors, accepted Marino's arguments. Consequently, Bayou's accounts that year showed a healthy profit, rather than a loss.

Bayou repeated the process the following year, but by 1998 the losses were too great to be disguised in this way. Marino and Israel came up with a new solution. Marino set up an apparently independent accounting firm, Richmond-Fairfield, which became Bayou's auditors. Marino then simply produced audited accounts falsely showing a good return for the year. This practice continued in subsequent years, until 2005, by which time investors are thought to have put a total of $450 million into what were now several hedge funds run by Bayou. Israel and Marino spent investors' money liberally on themselves, mostly channelling it through the commissions that the dealer–broker was now once again charging the hedge funds. Israel, dependent on painkillers, seems to have been losing his grip on reality and began to invest hedge fund money in increasingly bizarre and risky enterprises. In 2004 Israel sent $120 million to Germany as an investment in a highly dubious scheme offered to him by Robert Booth Nichols, who claimed to be a top secret agent. This was a final throw of the dice; in April, Israel and Marino had suspended the funds' trading and had transferred all the remaining money into an account from which they invested in crazy schemes, of which the Robert Booth Nichols's deal was the last.

In July 2005, Israel and Marino wrote to their investors telling them that the funds were being liquidated and they would soon receive the balances of their accounts. The next month investors received redemption cheques, but these bounced, and the SEC was called in. It was all over. Israel was sentenced to 20 years, jumped bail and tried unsuccessfully to fake his own death, receiving a further 2 years after his recapture.

A hedge fund analyst, Benjamin Deschaine, came across Bayou early in 1995 and undertook a 'due diligence' investigation of the fund to see if it would be of interest to his own firm's clients. The fact that Bayou's sister company acted as its broker, which Bayou freely admitted, was not a good sign. Deschaine tried to have meetings with Israel, and then Marino, but was fobbed off. He contacted people who had worked at a previous employer of Israel's, who said they had never heard of him (Israel had exaggerated the importance of his position at that firm). He then asked Bayou for a copy of their prospectus, and was told that the firm did not produce traditional offering documents, and instead gave investors a fact-finding questionnaire. Deschaine says that at this point he dropped the investigation; without suspecting fraud, he simply felt that something wasn't right.

Deschaine's investigation in Bayou was preliminary and superficial. If the fund had seemed worthwhile he would have followed up with a more thorough scrutiny that would no doubt have uncovered serious problems. The point is that he didn't need to; he had seen enough that didn't seem quite right to be happy to drop Bayou from his list. This straightforward research could have been carried out by any investor prepared to make a minimal effort. Time and again, in the history of fraud, we encounter stories of how other market professionals took a long, shrewd look at a fraudster and simply walked away. This is the investor's great trump card – if there is something that you don't like about the deal, you can just drop it and move on to find something you like better.

Bayou started out as a genuine hedge fund. By the law of averages, some hedge funds must make losses, and Bayou was one of them. This could be attributed to bad luck, or perhaps to poor judgement by Israel in following his trading program. Covering up the losses by rebating the dealing commissions would have worked if Israel had not continued to make more and more losses. The step into full-blown criminality occurred when Marino and Israel set up the phoney accounting firm to provide bogus independent audits of what now became entirely fraudulent accounts. For some eight years, Israel and Marino had sent regular statements, including a weekly electronic newsletter, to their investors, telling them they were making healthy returns. Nobody seems to have checked up on the auditor; a dedicated sleuth would surely have discovered that in some official records Marino was listed as a principal of Richmond-Fairfield. Further checks would have revealed that Israel had been involved in a string of lawsuits, including a conviction for drunk driving, and that he had massaged his employment history on his CV. None of this would necessarily have been damning evidence on its own, but together it should have at least raised eyebrows. What is striking about the Bayou case is that quite a number of other firms invested in Bayou, or put their clients on to it, without performing adequate due diligence.

Avoiding hedge fund fraud

Hedge funds are minimally regulated operations that are supposed only to accept investments from investors who are sufficiently financially sophisticated to understand the risks that they are taking. With the rapid growth of hedge funds, however, simply having enough money to invest seems to have become a sufficient qualification to actually be accepted as an investor. One Oxbridge professor and his wife, both deceased, lost a large part of their assets not long after retirement by investing in a hedge fund that (legitimately) failed; while they had enough money to invest and were intelligent people, they were certainly not sufficiently interested or knowledgeable about the risks involved to be judged as sufficiently financially sophisticated to become hedge fund investors.

> The UK's FSA believes that there is an increased likelihood of fraud in the hedge fund industry because of its light regulation, weaker controls, and high rewards for fund managers.

The UK's FSA believes that there is an increased likelihood of fraud in the hedge fund industry because of its light regulation, weaker controls, and high rewards for fund managers.

An FSA report highlights cases involving hiding losses, as with Bayou, and potential jurisdiction problems with hedge fund administrators, which are usually based offshore, and it is plain from the report that the lack of transparency in hedge funds provides a cover for managers to give false information to their investors about the value of their funds.

Although most hedge fund managers may be honest, there is clearly a heightened possibility of fraud in the industry, and the lack of transparency makes this difficult to quantify or detect. This is very unsatisfactory for a reasonably cautious investor. Nevertheless, the success of some hedge funds, and the evident talent of some hedge fund managers, can make this form of investment attractive (although overall, the long-term performance of hedge funds as a group is unimpressive). Investors who do decide to take the plunge must be prepared to undertake more due diligence than they would if they were investing in, say, a well-regulated unit trust. The due diligence will not provide complete protection, but in many cases, such as Bayou, the fraudsters do not completely cover their tracks, and some quite straightforward enquiries can reveal problems. There are also specialist firms that will undertake due diligence for you, for a fee, which might be worthwhile if your initial research uncovered any potential problems. At the very least, it is necessary to do the following.

- Read the prospectus and investment agreement carefully.

- Check that the assets the fund manages really exist.

- Check that the custodian of the fund's assets is genuinely independent from the fund managers.

- Verify that the auditor and lawyers for the fund are genuine. In particular, check that the auditor is independent, has extensive experience of auditing hedge funds, and the auditor's reports contain no qualifications to the accounts.

- Check regulators' websites for information about the fund and its managers.

- Check the references given by the fund managers – if possible, verify every entry in their CVs. Are they really qualified to pursue the investment strategies of the hedge fund?

- Read the financial statements carefully. Pay close attention to the valuations of illiquid or unusual assets. Look at the pattern of returns – having very few months with negative returns is a danger sign.

- Talk to as many different people in and around the firm as possible.

It may be we are living through a hedge fund mania that will look rather silly in hindsight. Certainly, the appearance of firms specialising in a complete service to help you set up your own hedge fund suggests that there are quite a number of unqualified people who think it would be a good idea to become hedge fund managers! The unusually high remuneration for managers does not seem justified for the majority of funds. The failure rate for new hedge funds is also high – it is estimated that 1 in 5 fail in their first year. The total returns for the period 2002–2012 has been only 17% for the average hedge fund, and there are concerns that the 2% fee plus 20% profit structure has enabled managers to line their own pockets excessively. The HFRX, an index widely used as a benchmark for hedge fund performance, has underperformed the S&P 500 for nine years out of the last ten (to late 2012).

This is not to suggest that the hedge fund industry may not transform itself in the future and achieve better results, as it did in the 1980s and 1990s. Given the lack of transparency and the greater risk of fraud, however, investors should approach hedge funds with caution, and undertake a thorough due diligence investigation before deciding to invest.

11

All the books are cooked: the trouble with company accounts

We don't break the law.

Kenneth Lay, CEO of Enron
(died in 2006 while awaiting sentencing for fraud)

Most of us don't realise that there are no universal standards of accounting, although there is currently an ongoing effort to persuade countries across the world to adopt and properly implement the 'International Financial Reporting Standards' (IFRS), which would go some way towards this goal. The lack of a universal standard makes it extremely difficult to compare the performance of apparently similar companies operating in different countries, or even in the same country. Much of what you read about ways to pick bargain shares by analysing their accounts only applies in the US, for instance. In this chapter we'll look at problems that arise when trying to interpret the accounts of publicly listed companies, and I'll suggest some guidelines for spotting questionable practices. I'll show how two very different publicly listed companies, Crazy Eddie and Enron, both produced false accounts for several years before finally unravelling.

Legal differences

Most private investors do not appreciate that the laws affecting shareholders' rights vary enormously around the world, and while London and Wall Street may have a broadly similar approach to public companies, much of the rest of the world does not. This fact has many complex and unexpected effects – for example, while you may be able to make some sense of the accounts produced by a company in the UK, you may be unaware that its subsidiary in, say, Brazil, is allowed to operate in ways not allowed in the UK, which could give you a distorted picture of the whole group.

Commercial law derives either from 'common law' (in the UK and much of the US) or from 'civil law' (itself derived from Roman law, common in much of Europe). Most of the newer, developed economies have taken their commercial law from one of these two sources, but via an intermediary system. For example, the laws governing the stock markets of Malaysia, Hong Kong and Singapore are based on English law, while those of South Korea and Japan are based on German law, and those of Brazil, Italy and Turkey are based on French law. These differences really matter; by and large, English law provides significantly better protection for small shareholders than do the other systems, while French law is generally thought to offer the least protection. For example, in the French system it is common for minority shareholders to have restricted voting rights.

Corporate governance from the investor's point of view

Warren Buffett often says he only likes to invest in companies that are honestly run and whose senior management comprises people of high integrity; and he often adds there aren't many such firms to be found. As investors we are swamped with material suggesting that companies are all honestly managed and it is easy to make direct comparisons between them. Neither of these notions is universally true; in fact, it is extremely difficult to make exact comparisons between companies even when their accounts are honest, and, as we have seen throughout this book, many companies do not produce honest accounts.

Modern listed companies survive in a maelstrom of codes and regulations, collectively known as 'corporate governance'. These include stock market regulations, voluntary codes of practice and other commercial laws. In theory, good corporate governance should enable companies to borrow money, issue shares, and strive to increase the value of their shareholders' investments while at the same time acting ethically and responsibly towards all other stakeholders and to the whole of society. That's quite a tall order. Business is a rough, tough, competitive world, and as investors we probably wouldn't mind too much if the CEOs of the companies we invest in were a bit rougher and tougher – and better at bending the rules – than their rivals, but that wouldn't be fair, would it? So is the solution, popular in these days of ongoing financial crisis, to string up every CEO for the tiniest infraction or to bring in the dead hand of government bureaucracy to tie up firms in a rigid system that prevents them from being able to make profits while the going is good?

> Modern listed companies survive in a maelstrom of codes and regulations, collectively known as 'corporate governance'.

Clearly, there needs to be a balance between regulation and freedom to act. Many would argue that the balance went too far towards freedom during the 'noughties', and this led directly to the banking crisis of 2007/8. In any case, it is clear, during boom times corporate governance tends to become more relaxed, and it is only after the inevitable bust that the really grotesque failures of corporate governance emerge and the public starts baying for blood. When times are good, investors seem not to want to look too deeply into how the companies they invest in are achieving their profits; but when times are bad, investors are extremely eager to know whom to blame for their losses.

The long-term trend towards globalisation, if it continues, makes corporate governance more important than ever. As China, India and other newly developed countries launch their megafirms on to the world's stock markets, the whole stock market system may be threatened if they do not conform to the norms of corporate governance, and this could be bad for everyone (this is not to ignore the multitude of corporate governance scandals that occur periodically in the long-established stock markets such as in the US and the UK). It is now widely recognised that there is a need for a bigger push towards better universal standards of corporate governance. In 1999, for example, the Organisation for Economic Cooperation and Development (OECD) issued the OECD Principles for Corporate Governance, which was ratified by its 29 members. These principles are worth considering in a little detail.

Transparency

Investors should receive enough information about the company for them to make informed decisions. For a publicly listed company, such information should be announced publicly to ensure that everyone gets the information at the same time.

Accountability

It should be clear who is responsible for corporate governance within a firm. There should be an effort to make the interests of investors and senior managers converge – this is often not the case.

Responsibility

Companies should obey the laws and regulations of the countries in which they do business. This might seem obvious, but think about what can happen when a large firm is the main employer in a poor country in, say, Africa or Latin America.

Fairness

Investors, especially minority shareholders and foreign shareholders, should be treated fairly.

To the outsider, these OECD principles might seem to be stating the obvious, but the fact is that they are open to interpretation, both honestly and dishonestly, and much depends upon the legal system in the country where the company operates, as mentioned above. In any case, they are far too general in themselves to help us, the small private investors.

Company accounts

'And now, it's spinach time!', as Warren Buffett wrote in the introduction to the accounting section of one of his annual reports. We all know we are supposed to look carefully at company accounts, but they are confusing and hard work, and it's so much easier just to place our bets and hope the share price goes up. In this chapter I'm going to assume that you know enough of the basics about publicly listed company accounts (which in principle are no different from small business accounts, or even household accounts) to be able to follow our tale of woe. If you don't know enough, before becoming an investor you should definitely read one of the many good books on corporate accounts that are widely available.

So, here goes. First, as mentioned at the beginning of this chapter, it is important to understand that there is no single, universally accepted theory of accounting, and accounting methods vary greatly between individual firms, industries and countries. This may be perfectly reasonable and cause no problems for firms themselves, but it makes it difficult for investors to understand accounts, and even more difficult for them to make comparisons between, say, firms or industries.

Accountants like to apply certain general principles that, though sensible in themselves, can raise really knotty problems and cause confusion among investors. These are the following.

Historic cost

Accountants like to value company assets at the price it cost the company to buy them. This is sensible, because it helps to prevent management from marking up their assets to ludicrous levels. However, what if the firm bought an office block in 1915 for £2,000 and it is now worth £25 million? Valuing it at cost would not present a true picture. For this reason, revaluations are allowed from time to time. The 'asset strippers' of the 1960s and 1970s exploited the historic cost principle by buying up old companies with massively undervalued assets and selling these assets off at a profit – hence the revaluation rule. As we will see, however, newer creative accounting methods, such as 'mark-to-market', have on occasion been misused in order to produce figures far in excess of those generated by the historic cost method.

Materiality

An independent auditor (accountant) can't check how every single paper clip has been used, so he or she is usually allowed to decide what is 'material', i.e. important, and what is 'immaterial', i.e. unimportant. This gives canny managers some scope for abuse, especially if they can bully or deceive the auditor, as in the case of Crazy Eddie (see below).

Conservatism

When in doubt, accountants will choose the most conservative number; for example, by accounting for losses as soon as they are foreseen. This often puts them into conflict with managers, who generally are trying to paint the best picture possible of their company's profits. Investors, often their own worst enemies, sometimes weigh in to try to influence valuations – for example, in bull markets, investors may campaign for optimistic valuations, and some accountancy firms may be willing to become ... well, less conservative, shall we say. A good accountant is a wise and wonderful creature – and no self-respecting crook wants one of *them* auditing his firm.

Substance

There are many, many ways to arrange things so that an important transaction doesn't appear on the books. Why would you want to do this?

You might want to avoid tax illegally by keeping profits low, for instance. Alternatively, you might want to hide the enormous debts you have accumulated so that your share price doesn't drop. Good accountants are supposed to prefer the 'substance' of the transaction over its 'form' and to prevent these manoeuvres.

Consistency

Accountants believe that companies shouldn't change their accounting methods and policies frequently. Occasionally a change may be justified, but it is considered a red flag when a company or group of companies does this often. Robert Maxwell, the owner of the Mirror Group of newspapers in the 1980s and 1990s, is known to have changed the reporting date of some of the companies in his group frequently, and by doing so to have deceived his auditors. Consistency helps investors compare like with like; if there has been a change, investors need to make sure that they understand the reasons for the change, and if these reasons are legitimate.

Realisation

Wise accountants think that you should record a profit when you have raised an invoice, or better still, when you have been paid. Sometimes they agree to record the profits on invoices issued, but make a 'provision' (i.e. a downward adjustment) in case full payment is not received. There is scope here for managerial deceit.

Going concern

Lastly, accountants assume that the company will keep going; thus, for example, the materials the company purchases will eventually be turned into finished products. If the company goes bust this will not happen – so the 'going concern' idea produces higher values than can be obtained if the company goes bust.

Canny managers, who may be upstanding individuals in all other ways, often try to exploit the difficulties that these accounting principles raise, and thus we can never be completely certain that we, the outside investors, are getting a true picture. But occasionally really ruthless crooks appear, whose *raison d'être* is to deceive outsiders about their accounts. They're more common than you might think, but the company we are going to look at first managed to do it so thoroughly, both as a private company and then as a publicly listed company, that it really deserves a prize for chicanery. Its name? Crazy Eddie Inc.

Crazy Eddie

Crazy Eddie Inc. was a chain of TV and electronics stores in New York, run by a close-knit family of Syrian origin. Established in the late 1960s, the company was well known in the New York area for its aggressive advertising – 'his prices are IN-SA-A-A-A-A-ANE!' – and by the 1980s it was being parodied on national television. In 1984 the firm went public, and within two years its share price had risen from $4.50 to $37.50, and, significantly, about half of its shares were owned by financial institutions. Wall Street liked Crazy Eddie. The price to earnings ratio was high at 39, but that was OK because Wall Street believed it was going to go on growing. Even from the publicly available information, there were some worrying aspects to Crazy Eddie.

> **Even from the publicly available information, there were some worrying aspects to Crazy Eddie.**

The firm's boss, Eddie Antar, employed a number of relatives in senior positions. The firm did not own its stores, but leased them, and some of these stores were leased from relatives of Eddie Antar. Crazy Eddie had done a lot of business with companies owned by relatives of Eddie Antar, and the firm had made loans to some of these individuals. Crazy Eddie had also made substantial loans to employees of the company, some of whom were relatives of Eddie Antar. Furthermore, some of the Antars employed by the firm had rather generous stock option plans. So, why should any of this worry an investor? Because all this was *prima facie* evidence that Eddie might have been working in the interests of his family rather than the interests of the shareholders.

In 1986 the firm announced that it was getting into the TV home-shopping business, and the share price shot up to $40. Wall Street analysts continued to foresee great things. In October 1986 there was a profits warning. In January 1987 Eddie Antar resigned as CEO. The share price dropped to $10, and by the spring it had become clear that the firm wasn't growing. In May Eddie launched a takeover bid, offering $7 per share, but was outbid by another wheeler-dealer, Elias Zinn. Zinn acquired the firm in November 1987, and promptly audited the firm's stock, only to find that some $65 million worth of stock was absent (this was later revised up to $80 million). Zinn claimed that Eddie Antar had produced false accounts.

As the firm collapsed, Eddie Antar went into hiding in Israel. In 1993 he was extradited from Israel to the US, and in 1994 he was sentenced to $12\frac{1}{2}$ years in prison for racketeering and fraud. This was overturned, but in a 1997 trial he was sentenced to eight years in prison and ordered to pay $150 million in fines. Various other lawsuits are ongoing.

What's interesting about this case is the detail. Crazy Eddie was found to have recorded fictitious sales, made its employees lie to the auditors, borrowed stock from suppliers to exaggerate its inventory, concealed debts, and changed auditors' notes without their knowledge. Pretty good going!

Here's how they did it. Sam Antar is a relative of Eddie Antar, the firm's boss. Sam served as Crazy Eddie's Chief Financial Officer and was convicted for three felonies relating to the firm, but served no jail time as the result of a plea bargain. In recent years he has set up as an adviser to government agencies investigating fraud, and has produced extensive analysis of the various fraudulent practices that occurred at Crazy Eddie. His descriptions of them are instructive. Many of the methods used are well-known 'hardy perennials', and can be easily detected; however, the ways in which Sam and other insiders managed to conceal the frauds provide useful insights into how relatively simple wrongdoing can evolve into a complex web of deceit that fooled thousands of stock market investors.

According to Sam Antar, the Crazy Eddie saga had three distinct phases: an initial decade (1969–1979) when the company was privately owned by the family, during which efforts were focused on illegally under-reporting profits and failing to record employee payments in order to avoid taxation; a second phase, from 1980 to 1984, when the family reduced the under-reporting of profits, thereby creating the impression of additional profit growth, in preparation for floating the company on the stock market; and a final phase from 1985 to 1987, during which company insiders sought to inflate reported profits and disguise liabilities, thereby boosting the company's share price. Sam Antar claims that there was a decision to float the company on the stock market because the potential fraudulent gains were much larger. By inflating the profits of the public company, the earnings per share (EPS) could be increased. The EPS is an important investment measure. As the EPS increases, the company's share price will also tend to increase, enabling major shareholders to offload shares at a higher price.

As a young accountant, Sam Antar went to work for Crazy Eddie's external auditors, while secretly also working for Crazy Eddie, with the explicit intention of learning how to 'take advantage' of the auditors. In 1979, Crazie Eddie's owners pocketed some $3 million in unrecorded cash income (known as 'skimming'), but in preparation for going public the skimming was reduced over the next few years, reaching zero by 1984. This had the effect of making it appear that Crazy Eddie was growing during the period, when in fact its profits and income had been stagnant. Employees who had previously been paid mainly in cash off the books to avoid payroll taxes were now included in the accounts, at their full salaries, including payroll taxes. This sudden leap in the cost of salaries was explained away as being a reward for success.

In September 1984 Crazy Eddie went public at $8 a share. Company insiders retained significant stock holdings in the company, and stood to gain if the share price rose and they could offload their shares at a higher price. According to Sam Antar, members of the Antar family were able to sell $90 million worth of their personal holdings during the next three years as they successfully managed to boost the share price by fraudulent means.

How was this done? After all, the stock market has very elaborate structures and rules to prevent exactly this kind of fraud from occurring. For example, public companies must have independent auditors, and if they do not use one of the large, well-established accounting firms they are regarded with suspicion.

When it went public, Crazy Eddie switched to the large firm Peat Marwick Main (now KPMG), an entirely normal move when a private company goes public. Like other large firms, Peat Marwick used junior staff to do the donkey work for the annual audit. According to Sam Antar, these individuals – and their immediate supervisors – were all under 30. They could be distracted. Antar claims that he conducted a calculated programme of subversion, encouraging Crazy Eddie employees to become as friendly as possible with the auditors, constantly taking them out for meals at the company's expense, while Sam himself took out the more senior supervisors to glamorous bars. Antar claims that this method had two effects: first, the auditors were genuinely taken in by the charm offensive and came to believe that Eddie and his staff were honest and likeable; and second, these social activities had the effect of drastically slowing down the auditing process. The audit, lasting eight weeks, took place once a year, and the more the auditors' work was slowed down, the more information they would have to take on faith, rather than checking it for themselves.

Early in 1986, company insiders wanted to issue more shares to the public, and at the same time to sell some $20 million of their own shares. For this to work, the company's quarterly figures had to meet or exceed Wall Street analysts' predictions for the growth in sales. Analysts had predicted a 10% growth in 'same-store' sales (i.e. sales in long-established stores, rather than in newly opened stores), but the Antars knew that the quarterly figures they were about to announce would show that same-store sales had only grown by 4%. They had to make it look as if same-store sales had grown by 10% if they were to have a successful share issue. To achieve this, the family brought back some $2 million dollars from secret overseas bank accounts (this money had been accumulated from off-the-books cash sales during the private company phase) and deposited it in Crazy Eddie's accounts, making it look as if it was the proceeds from current sales. They didn't try very hard; Sam claims that the company didn't even take the trouble to create false sales invoices to explain the deposits of the overseas money (which were in the form of bank drafts worth tens of thousands of dollars each). Moreover, the overseas money was deposited all at once, which made it appear that the majority of same-store sales had occurred in the last two days of the financial year, a very unlikely occurrence and one that should have alerted auditors to the problem.

Sam claims that on this occasion his calculated plan to distract the junior auditing staff succeeded in slowing their work to the extent that there was no time for them to make the various checks that would have uncovered this fraudulent injection of cash into the company. The new issue of shares went well, and Eddie Antar and his father (also named Sam) sold some of their own shares; because Crazy Eddie had met analysts' projections, the share price had increased, and the Antars collected $24.3 million for their shares, rather than the $20 million they had expected. Thus, by secretly returning $2 million of their illegally gained profits, they had not only ensured the success of the share issue and the sale of their own shares, but had also more than covered the $2 million they had had to put in to the company.

'Ah,' you may be thinking, 'this kind of thing may have gone on back in the 1970s and 1980s in the mean streets of New York, but it is not common now. Most firms, both private and public, have genuine accounts.' If you believe this, you need to revise your views. Firms have considerable leeway in how they present their accounts, and there is ample opportunity for companies, small and large, to commit such egregious frauds.

Let's look now at a much more substantial company that not only committed accounting fraud involving billions of dollars but also brought about the collapse of its auditors, Arthur Andersen, then one of the 'big five' worldwide accounting firms. This was Enron, a global giant that was a major player in an international derivatives market for gas, oil, electricity, broadband communications and other commodities.

Enron

Enron's CEO, Kenneth Lay, had built the firm up from a local seller of gas and electricity in Texas in the 1980s into the US's seventh-largest company by 2001. Its business was very complex – mystifying to many outsiders

– but in early 2001 Enron looked like a very solid company indeed, and its bonds were rated AAA (S&P's top investment grade). In hindsight, its annual report for 2000 makes interesting reading. In the financial highlights section, its total sales are given as a staggering $100.789 billion, with a net income of $1.266 billion. Over ten years, the S&P 500 index had produced a total return of 383%, dwarfed by Enron's total return of 1,415% over the same period. A reader might have experienced a little twinge of doubt, though, when looking over the sales figures in previous years – just over $100 billion in 2000, up from some $40 billion in 1999, $32 billion in 1998, and $20 billion in 1997. How can any company achieve such an extraordinary growth in sales?

Enron's explanation was superficially convincing – it was all to do with being in the right place at the right time in newly deregulated markets, such as energy, and in entirely new markets, such as broadband. Enron had 'networks of strategic assets', 'unparalleled liquidity and market-making abilities', and 'innovative technology' that enabled it to beat the competition in the wholesale markets across the world. All these markets were set to grow massively over the next few years, and Enron was going to get a bigger piece of the pie. It had operations all over the world – including Japan, Singapore, Europe and Australia. It had more than 20,000 employees, 38 power stations, a host of pipelines in the Americas, gas extraction plants, paper mills, oil exploration companies … in short, Enron was big, really big, and it said it was going to go on growing. The firm had reported that it was on track to double its sales figures in 2001, which would have made it the largest, or second-largest, corporation in the whole world in terms of sales.

It's easy to be wise after the event, but a *Forbes* magazine article of 2002, the year after Enron had begun to collapse, points out that it was rather extraordinary for a firm with only 20,000 employees to be able to generate sales on a similar scale to those of Citigroup (238,000 employees), General Electric (312,000 employees) and IBM (312,000 employees). Looked at another way, firms with a similar number of employees to Enron were unable to achieve anything like Enron's sales figures, such as Texaco ($50 billion) and Goldman Sachs ($33 billion).

People who believed in Enron were very excited about a notion known as 'the "New Economy"'. The New Economy was all about being ... well, it was never quite clear what the New Economy was really all about, but there was a lot of talk about 'business models' (which often seems to be code for 'We have no idea how we are going to make money'), the power of the internet, the increase in globalisation and free markets, the opportunities in derivatives thanks to the new methods of valuing them, and so on. In short, it was all achingly hip – this was the time of the internet bubble, remember – and, as Jeff Skilling, who had joined Enron in 1990 and took over the top job from Kenneth Lay early in 2001, used to say, you either get it, or you don't. But Enron wasn't some fly-by-night internet start-up, it was a genuinely massive firm, so if its boss thought there was such a thing as the New Economy it was not unreasonable, perhaps, to give him the benefit of the doubt. Skilling and other Enron managers were talking about the firm being 'asset-less' – a classic New Economy phrase – because it dealt in 'risk-intermediation', providing services to customers to hedge the risks of price fluctuations in the underlying commodities it dealt in. In actual fact, however, Enron was not asset-less at all. As we have seen, it owned a large number of assets, in which it had invested rapidly during the preceding five years, and many of these assets were not generating profits. Indeed, some of Enron's investments, including Wessex Water in the UK, an Indian power plant, and a curious power plant mounted on a barge next to a hotel in the Dominican Republic, were losing very substantial sums of money.

> People who believed in Enron were very excited about a notion known as 'the "New Economy"'.

Then, in April 2001, Skilling decided to hold a conference call with stock market analysts and financial reporters. During the call a hedge fund manager, Richard Grubman, pressed Skilling to provide a quarterly balance sheet along with the earnings statement Enron had announced, at which Skilling called Grubman an 'asshole'. This unCEO-like behaviour was widely reported at the time, and has since become an iconic example of corporate arrogance. Perhaps we should not judge Skilling too harshly for the outburst (he apparently was aware that Grubman was short-selling Enron stock on a large scale), but the question, innocent or not, must have touched a nerve, as Skilling was well aware at the time that Enron was hiding massive debts.

So how did it all happen? Unlike Crazy Eddie, the shenanigans at Enron were not a case of a tightly knit family setting out to commit a long-term fraud from the outset. It seems that rather than being entirely pre-planned, senior management in Enron became progressively enmeshed in a truly complex web of deceit as many of its elaborate profit-making ventures gradually began to go wrong. The deregulation of utilities industries around the world during the 1980s and 1990s had presented a genuine opportunity for Enron to expand, and Kenneth Lay was truly an industry expert – he had actually been an energy regulator for the US government in the 1970s. The idea of becoming a market maker in a host of energy and commodity industries seems to have been pushed by Skilling during the 1990s, rather than by Lay. By arguing that Enron had created new trading markets in these commodities, Skilling was able to persuade accountants that it was appropriate to use 'mark-to-market' accounting. Mark-to-market accounting is very complicated but briefly it is where the total profit that Enron would make on a contract would be recognised when the contract was first signed – hitherto the firm had used a traditional historic cost approach (see page 159), where actual costs and revenues were booked as they occurred. Enron was heavily involved in derivatives, where mark-to-market methods are problematic because there is often no way to validate estimates of true market values. To estimate the values, Enron had to make very complex assumptions – which, with the best will in the world, might be wrong – about such things as future demand, future interest rates, and future variation in prices. It seems that Enron had an understandable tendency to make rather optimistic assumptions in these matters, which tended to improve its earnings figures.

Mark-to-market alone might be forgivable, but Enron was up to other tricks, too. It was using a legal loophole to report the total sales value of its derivative deals as income, which dramatically inflated its sales figures. Enron's proprietary trading platform, Enron Online, allowed other parties to trade in energy and commodities, with Enron taking a small cut of each transaction. Normally such an operation would be accounted for on the 'agent' model, where the value of the fees would be reported, but not the entire value of the transaction – Goldman Sachs and other firms with trading systems use this accounting model. But because Enron could argue that it owned or controlled the items being traded, it was able to use the 'merchant' model, reporting the entire value of the cost and sale value of each transaction, which had the effect of vastly increasing the firm's sales figures. This, of course, did not increase the profit figures, but in the fast-paced world of the New Economy it appeared all that would improve later – the name of the game was to grab as large a chunk of the business as possible. According to some estimates, if Enron had not used mark-to-market and the merchant model, its 2000 sales figures would not have been the $100.789 billion, but a paltry $6.3 billion.

It also emerged later that Enron had been using a large number of offshore companies called Special Purpose Entities (SPEs) to hide massive losses, claim more than $1 billion in fictitious earnings, and to adjust the point when income was recognised as having been received in order to 'manage earnings' in line with analysts' expectations. The SPEs were in effect a means to keep much of Enron's activities 'off-balance sheet', away from the prying eyes of Wall Street analysts.

During mid-2001 Skilling sold $33 million worth of his own shares in Enron, and then resigned from the company in August. Kenneth Lay tried to reassure Wall Street that nothing was wrong, but the share price continued to drop, as it had been during the early part of the year. Analysts had begun to ask too many awkward questions. In February, for instance, a report from John S. Herold Inc. expressed doubts about Enron's profitability, and wondered if the company could keep its position as market leader in the energy industry. In March an article in *Fortune* magazine suggested that Enron's share price might be too high. In October Enron began to sell some assets, and then announced that it had suffered a $1 billion loss in non-recurring expenses. In November the dam finally burst; Enron revealed that it had overstated its earnings by just under $600 million, and it owed $3 billion to its SPEs. Its AAA bonds were drastically downgraded and the SEC began a formal investigation. Enron went bust, leaving thousands of employees with no job and having lost their savings in Enron share purchase plans. Soon, the SEC sued Arthur Andersen, Enron's auditors. Employees of the massive accountancy firm were eventually convicted of deliberately shredding Enron-related documents in an effort to obstruct justice, which severely damaged the firm's reputation. Arthur Andersen surrendered its accountancy licences in 2002 and went out of business. After a long trial Jeff Skilling was sentenced to 24 years in prison for securities fraud. Kenneth Lay was also convicted of securities fraud but died of a heart attack before sentencing.

In the grand regulatory tradition of shutting the stable door after the horse has bolted, in 2002 US Congress introduced the Sarbanes–Oxley Act, which, in the words of one researcher, 'is a mirror image of Enron: the company's perceived corporate governance failings are matched virtually point-for-point in the principal provisions of the Act.' Well, the government has to be seen to be doing something when a scandal of this magnitude occurs, but Sarbanes–Oxley, or 'SOX', has attracted much criticism in recent years for having a damping effect on business in the US. More importantly, SOX was completely unable to prevent the next big scandal in the US, the sub-prime mortgage scandal – in which the wrongdoing involved lending too much money to the wrong people, rather than, as in the case of Enron, pretending to be making more money than it actually was. The point is that there are a million ways to cheat the public, and producing legislation as a knee-jerk reaction to the last crisis is very unlikely to anticipate the next crisis, which usually appears in a different form; in other words, new regulations tend to learn the wrong lessons from a major scandal.

Enron was a massive failure of corporate governance. It was *the* hot firm at a time when the US was both excited about the potential offered by the internet and globalisation, and worried about the rise of China as a manufacturing power. Wall Street could and should have known better: if expert analysts can't really understand a company's accounts, it's usually not a good sign, but Wall Street went along for several years with the idea that Enron was a fabulously innovative firm heading for stardom. Although it was never fully established how Arthur Andersen came to approve Enron's highly questionable accounting methods, it seems likely that this was a case of trying to observe the letter, rather than the spirit, of the law. The accountancy firm had quite an incentive not to make waves – in 2001 alone, it received $25 million in auditing fees and $27 million in consultancy fees.

Investors and accounts

So what can we learn from all this as investors? Three things are clear.

1 Wall Street analysts often ignore warning signs about a company that is in fashion. As investors, we cannot rely absolutely on the material put out by analysts; we need to use our own capacity for critical thinking. Businesses are real things, run by real people. In the case of Crazy Eddie, it would not have been easy for a private investor to detect fraud in the firm; however, Sam Antar argues that anyone who had carefully read the footnotes of the company's reports would have seen that Crazy Eddie had poor internal accounting controls. Furthermore, Barron's magazine had published a sceptical article about the firm before it went public, and in its filings to the SEC (publicly available) it was quite plain that many members of the Antar family had been involved in 'related party dealings' with the firm, including, for example, a large loan to a medical school in St Lucia in which family members had shares. In short, there was sufficient information available, if anyone had chosen to look, to suggest that Crazy Eddie was not all that it should have been. As for the Wall Street hype surrounding Enron, you could either believe, as many did, that the 'New Economy' was going to sweep all before it without any casualties along the way, or you could choose not to do so. The obvious issue with Enron was its ridiculously rapid growth in sales at the same time as its percentage of profit was declining. Ultimately, whether or not you chose to believe the explanations proffered depended on your personal judgement, and it was not possible for an outsider to penetrate the accounts provided – but that in itself is

a warning sign. The moral? If you can't understand the accounts, don't invest! Don't rely on the analysts to do the work for you.

2 Corporate governance really does matter, but it only really works if the principals involved – the people running the company – are sincerely trying to implement corporate governance properly. For example, it was plain long before its collapse that Enron's accounts were not transparent, and its sexy creative accounting methods, such as mark-to-market and SPEs, which were mentioned in its annual reports, should have raised eyebrows among eagle-eyed investors. Company accounts can be sufficiently transparent without giving away trade secrets – and senior managers do have the power to make accounts transparent if they wish to do so. Senior managers at Enron evidently did not wish to do so. With Crazy Eddie, the mere fact that there were poor internal controls and extensive related-party transactions – both reported publicly – should have been enough to make an investor wonder if the firm's management were really committed to good corporate governance.

3 Investors cannot rely on auditors' opinions. They should be able to do so – that's what auditors are there for – but history has demonstrated that auditors have, on occasion, approved fraudulent accounts in very large firms, for reasons about which, sadly, we can usually only speculate. That Crazy Eddie, a much smaller firm than Enron, was able to fool its auditors is more surprising; thanks to Sam Antar, we now have a detailed account of how this was done (employees even went so far as to climb up ladders during stock checks to save the auditors the trouble, and then shouted down exaggerated numbers of the goods sitting on the high shelves, according to Antar). For the private investor, the frequent failures of auditors are a real problem – the whole market system relies on accurate information to function – but all is not lost. The art of assessing a company depends not only upon trying to understand its accounts, but also upon triangulation: cross-checking the information against managers' statements, company activities, news reports and even talking to company employees. You don't have to do

this with every company on the stock market – just the ones that seem interesting, and 'smell right'.

If you don't have the interest or ability to do this kind of digging, then you will have to rely on the opinions of others about the quality of particular companies and, as we have seen, the opinions of others, even professionals, may be wrong. This doesn't mean that you should avoid financial investment altogether, but it probably does mean you should avoid investing directly in individual companies – stick to index trackers, investment trusts and other forms of collective investment.

12

Safer strategies

The only function of economic forecasting is to
make astrology look respectable.

J.K. Galbraith

For most people, there can be few things worse than waking up one morning to discover that most or all of your wealth has disappeared through fraud, with little prospect of recovery. But in so many of the cases discussed in this book, the victims could have avoided or significantly reduced the risk of a massive loss by following well-established investment strategies and procedures. In this chapter we will look at how you can do this.

Even though as investors we must rely on the expertise of others in so many ways to be able to participate in the financial markets, we still need to take precautions ourselves. We cannot expect the government or the regulators to abolish all possibility of fraud – this is just unrealistic, given the massive growth and ever-increasing complexity of financial activity around the world during the last few decades.

There's an old story, perhaps from the 1920s, about a man who writes an angry letter to a railway company complaining that he has caught fleas by travelling on its trains. In due course he receives a letter of abject apology from the managing director, assuring him that this never ever happened before and it will be investigated thoroughly – but someone has accidentally included his original letter of complaint in the envelope. Across the top of his complaint letter the managing director has scrawled: 'send standard flea letter'. Today there is a widespread feeling, especially in the US, that the authorities are doing much the same in dealing with an industry that has got out of control and severely disrupted the global economy, but have the regulators really become less effective than they used to be? During a Senate hearing on the Madoff affair, Senator Charles Schumer remarked, 'When I got to Congress in 1980, the SEC was one of the premier organisations in the government ... Wow has it gone downhill!' I think he is right; back in the 1980s, for instance, the SEC was notorious for its overly aggressive pursuit of financial wrongdoing. The situation in the UK is a little different; for example, in the days when the Department of Trade and Industry (DTI) was responsible for preventing chicanery by company directors, people in the City used to call it 'the Department of Timidity and Inaction'.

In their defence, the regulators have much more to contend with than ever before, simply because of the massive growth of financial markets. The SEC claims that it receives hundreds of letters every day denouncing financial firms, and it is swamped. In the UK, the FSA is clearly spread too thin, trying to cover every aspect of financial activity that could affect the public while at the same time trying to fight large institutions with huge resources and essentially they don't really want to play ball. People who work in the City of London often say privately that compliance is a joke (financial firms have to employ special compliance officers who are supposed to police their activities). It's understandable, in a way; in the high-octane, amoral atmosphere of the markets, who do you listen to? Your boss who is screaming at you to make more money, or the hall monitor? There is a natural gamekeeper–poacher dynamic between regulators and moneymakers that is never going to go away. We investors need to recognise this. We must take advantage of every service and protection scheme that the regulators provide (and to be fair, they do provide a lot that is useful) but we have to remember they are only civil servants – if you want to see what some of them are like in person, you can watch the many hours of SEC testimony at Congressional hearings available on C-SPAN, an excellent not-for-profit public service network in the US that provides unfiltered TV recordings of these and similar events (at: **www.c-span.org**).

The first line of defence against fraud

If you find an investment that you feel comfortable with, it may be very tempting to park all your money in it, stop worrying about it and get on with your life. This is unwise, because if the investment goes bad for any reason, you may lose everything. Time and again in investment scandals we hear of people who 'lost their entire life's savings' in a single investment. Sometimes this is a journalistic exaggeration. The actor Kevin Bacon, for example, was reported as having lost everything in the Madoff fraud, but he has subsequently explained that he had only lost the majority of his financial assets, and still retained other assets, such as his home. So we need to be clear about what we mean by 'life's savings'; does it just mean your cash and near-cash savings, or all your financial assets, or your entire net worth that you have built up over a lifetime of work, including your house and your pension rights? Most often, people seem to be referring to the financial assets over which they have direct control when they say 'life's savings', excluding other valuable assets such as property and a pension. So if you are living in a £1 million house and you lose £100,000 in a fraud and have no cash left, you are clearly not as badly off as someone who sold their £1 million house and put everything, £1.1 million, into an investment that collapsed. There are other considerations, too. If you lose everything when you are 20, you have a lifetime to earn some more, but if you are old or sick, you may have no hope of escaping penury.

In 2009 a retired British soldier, Major William Foxton OBE, who had lost an arm on active service, shot himself after reportedly losing his 'life's savings' in two hedge funds that had invested with Madoff. The full financial details in this tragic case have not been divulged – and it is none of our business – but perhaps we can hope that Major Foxton owned a house and was in receipt of a pension, and that these had not been lost. Nevertheless, we can suppose that a very substantial percentage of his net worth had been lost in the Madoff affair. But investing all your financial assets in two funds is not a lot better than investing it all in only one fund, and in this particular case, the two funds appear to have flowed into the same black hole with Madoff.

Unless you love to take insane risks, if you ever lose a very large part of your wealth in a single fraud it will usually be one that you did not antici-pate. The fraud that gets you is the one you didn't see coming.

> The fraud that gets you is the one you didn't see coming.

So it makes no sense at all to put all your financial assets into one or two investments, unless you are just starting out and only have a very small sum to invest. Nor, incidentally, does it make sense to have all your wealth exclu-sively in financial assets (see 'Asset allocation', below). You need to spread your wealth across different investments to reduce the risk of being wiped out by a major fraud.

Investment advisers talk a lot about diversification, but in general they are focusing on how diversification reduces other kinds of risk. The trou-ble with fraud risk is that it can happen anywhere in the process, and the investment advice industry doesn't like to talk too loudly about it, because it frightens customers away. Regulators such as the FSA and the SEC do provide useful guidance on fraud prevention on their websites, though, and it is worth reviewing this material at regular intervals because new scams are always popping up.

So, how much should we diversify our financial investments? The stand-ard answer for direct investment in individual shares is that investing in 12 to 18 different companies is sufficient, but most people don't like to invest in individual shares; they like funds. Funds are supposed to have all kinds of benefits, including good diversification, but with the growth of hedge funds and other exotic types of funds in recent years the picture is becom-ing ever more complex and, as we have seen, the majority of funds do not perform particularly well in the long term (in fact, many funds don't even last very long before they are closed down). In the current environment there also seems to be a substantial increase in the risk of fraud in the fund

universe, which is very disturbing. If you are going to invest in funds, therefore, it may be sensible to spread the fraud risk by investing in several funds,
not just one or two, and to ensure that these funds are not closely associated with each other (for example, make sure that they are not all owned by
the same institution).

One way to look at this problem is to say to yourself, 'in the unlikely
event that one of my investments goes belly up because of fraud, what
percentage of my net worth can I stand to lose?' Saying '0%' is not an
acceptable answer, because there is always some risk, however small, of
fraud in any financial investment. Suppose you had invested only 10% of
your financial assets in Madoff; the loss would have been nasty, but it really
wouldn't have been the end of the world. You might even feel rather happy
about it, considering that so many other people lost so much more. I was
caught out during the dotcom boom when I put £10,000 into Marconi,
a telecoms and aerospace conglomerate. The price doubled within a fort-
night, and I should have sold, but I didn't. Within months the company
had collapsed and the shares were suspended. Two years later, after the
company was 'restructured' (essentially, it was taken over by its creditors
who received 99.5% of the new shares), I was sent a cheque for, if I recall
correctly, £1.50. These things happen. Although it was very annoying (I
still suspect wrongdoing) the money I lost was a small proportion of my
overall assets, so it did not destroy my life.

It is a good approach to spread your investments around to the
point where one of them failing isn't going to ruin your life, but it isn't
quite enough. Consider this: suppose you put all your investments
through one single adviser, or only buy products from one massive bank.
You could be back to square one if your adviser embezzles the money or
the bank collapses.

The answer is to conduct a careful risk assessment just for the possibility of collapse due to fraud. If you work in the UK, you may well have
encountered health and safety risk assessments at work, and these can be
usefully adapted for this purpose. For example, in a workplace health and
safety risk assessment the first thing you have to do is identify the hazards
by walking around the office looking for things that might hurt people

– you can do something similar by mentally walking through all the different organisations and processes involved in your investments. You can evaluate the risks you identify, rank them in order of the harm they could do to your wealth, and assess the measures you can take to prevent them or mitigate their effects. You should include all the investor protections provided by regulators and compensation schemes, so, for instance, you would note that your cash deposits in a UK high street bank are, at the time of writing, protected up to £85,000 by the Financial Services Compensation Scheme. There are some foreign banks in the UK that are not covered by the scheme, so you need to look at the details of the scheme on the FSA's website to make sure you are covered. Icesave, the Icelandic online savings outfit, was not covered by the scheme when it went bust. Write it all down on a risk assessment form and keep it – it's amazing how often little details change. Review your risk assessment form periodically and update it. This may seem boring and bureaucratic, but financial investment is all about the little details. If you get the little details wrong you can lose out badly, so take the trouble to do a good job. Incidentally, just because there is a compensation scheme it doesn't necessarily mean you'll get your money back quickly, so include that problem too in your assessment.

Lower your expectations

Many of us have a completely unrealistic idea about what kind of returns can be achieved on the stock market, or in financial investments generally. This is partly because people who work in finance seem to earn so much money; we never stop hearing about twenty-somethings being given an annual bonus that could buy a substantial house outright. It is a misleading picture, because many financial workers are paid much more modestly. Traders, especially derivatives traders are highly paid and often young; typically they start out (currently) on a salary of £30,000–£45,000

> Many of them don't make it, either because they are fired or because they can't stand the work any more.

and don't earn the really big bucks until they have much more experience. Many of them don't make it, either because they are fired or because they can't stand the work any more.

Elsewhere in the industry, it is really the fund managers and senior executives who make the big money. Much of this money is derived from the charges they impose for managing money, and not really from investment success. Consider a fund that is set up by a large institution to give ordinary investors the opportunity to participate in a sudden economic boom in, let's say, Ruritania. The fund runs for a few years, performs poorly, and when the Ruritanian economy collapses the fund is quietly shut down or merged with another fund. The managers have probably been paid very well – out of investors' money – to deliver very unimpressive results. In short, much of the big money earned by finance professionals comes from managing other people's money, and not from investment success. And all too often, as became clear in the sub-prime crisis in the US in 2007, finance professionals have been paid very well to operate dishonest schemes that eventually collapse. It is not really investment success, for example, to sell a lot of mortgages to people who can't afford them and will eventually default, or to bundle those toxic mortgages with other assets and then sell them much too expensively to other investors, especially if these practices bring down the whole sector and set off a major worldwide crisis lasting for years.

Another reason why many people have unrealistic expectations about investing in shares is they constantly hear stories about a particular share that has gone through the roof. If you look at the historic chart of such a share price, you see that at times, sometimes for years, the price has just gone up and up and it is easy to think you could have jumped in at a low point and jumped out at a high point with a huge profit. This is indeed possible on some occasions, but many studies show that overall this approach, which is a primitive form of market timing, does not produce good results. Furthermore, as outsiders, private investors have to pay much higher transaction costs than the professionals do, so frequent buying and selling will tend to bring your overall returns down.

So what kind of returns can we really expect if we take a sober, long-term approach to investing in equities (shares)? One famous study by Elroy, Dimson and Marsh finds that over the very long term, for example 1900–2011, most industrialised economies have generated a positive real return in their stock markets, but the average annual real rate of return has been quite low – in the region of 5%. This includes many years when returns have been negative, so in practice if you bought and held a representative sample of a stock market, for instance through an index tracking fund, you would find that in some years you got a much higher return and in some years you would have 'lost' money as prices dropped from the previous year's level – this is why investors in shares are advised to hold for as long as possible, to iron out the ups and downs. This is all actually quite good news, especially as the long-term return from bonds has been considerably lower, and in some cases has been negative. Over the very long term, then, equities have proved to be the best-performing financial asset type.

Many people scoff at the idea of only being able to obtain an average annual real return of 4% or 5% over the long run, but this is the level that pension funds, which are generally conservatively managed, tend to aim for. Of course, there are times when you make more, but there are also times when shares do very badly; share prices are 'volatile' (they go up and down unpredictably).

If you want to achieve a better return, you have to take on more risk by investing in shares that are much more volatile than the average. This is all very well, but share investing is not like playing a computer game when you can restart if things go wrong. If you invest for, say, 20 years in risky shares, you may do unusually well, but you may also do very badly indeed, and if that happens you can't undo your losses.

You can find a fuller discussion of these matters in my book *How the Stock Market Really Works*. For our present purposes, the bottom line is that lowered expectations and a long-term conservative outlook will help protect you psychologically from many of the temptations of investment, both fraudulent and otherwise.

Asset allocation

Asset allocation is an important concept for private investors. It is fairly plain that most of the people who lose their 'life's savings' in a fraud do not practise asset allocation effectively, if at all, so it is worthwhile learning something about it.

Asset allocation is all about looking at your whole wealth as one big pot, and considering how to divide it between different types of investments with the aim of getting the best return overall without taking more risk than you can handle. One of the most surprising features of careful asset allocation, which has been refined in recent years, is that it is possible to use it to obtain the same or better returns at a lower level of risk than if you just put all your money into equities. Using asset allocation you can achieve smoother, steadier returns than you could otherwise (another way to say this is that the returns have low volatility). One of the big attractions to investors of Madoff's scheme, remember, was that he claimed to be generating very stable returns. While asset allocation cannot actually produce the same degree of low volatility as Madoff was pretending to achieve, it can definitely take your returns in that direction.

> Asset allocation is all about looking at your whole wealth as one big pot

This is done by exploiting the fact that different types of asset (such as shares, buildings, bonds and commodities) tend to have a low correlation with one another. For instance, sometimes bonds will be performing quite well, while shares are performing very badly, and at other times the opposite will occur. The correct mixture of shares and bonds alone can lower the volatility (which is a proxy for risk) in a portfolio, and you can achieve even better results by carefully selecting a wider range of asset types in different countries, currencies and markets that are negatively correlated with one another.

The technicalities of how best to do this require specialist expertise and a knowledge of your specific personal circumstances. Sadly, the more ruthless financial professionals are ahead of you, and may try to confuse you by offering products that are supposed to give you this kind of low volatility but in actual fact do not.

Also, the theory tells us that you have to 'rebalance' your asset allocation every so often because over time elements in your portfolio will have grown at different rates, altering your risk exposure. To rebalance, you sell some investments in some asset classes and buy them in other asset classes to bring your portfolio back in line with your original asset allocations and keep the risk steady. One benefit of this is that when you rebalance you tend to sell investments when prices are high. There is one thing to watch out for – an unscrupulous adviser who tries to rebalance your portfolio too often to generate fees. This is called 'churning', and although churning is not permitted by the regulators, it is very hard to prove, so be careful in your choice of adviser.

If this approach seems interesting, you can find out much more from the work of Dr Craig Israelsen, an Associate Professor at Brigham Young University in Utah who is a leading expert on asset allocation for private investors in the US. He is also an extremely clever, humble and honest man, which makes a very nice change from the dreary bunch of finance professionals that so many of us have to contend with. For more information, see his website (at: **www.7twelveportfolio.com**).

Staying sane in the investment jungle

There is plenty that we investors can do to reduce the risk of suffering a damaging loss through fraud, and we owe it to ourselves to do as much as we can. Too many investors focus all their time on how to get the best return; we should spend at least as much time on figuring out how to reduce the risks, not only of outright fraud but also of all the other factors that can lead to investment losses. We need to keep on educating ourselves on financial matters, and to learn from a wide range of sources, not just our favourite newspaper and the TV news, but we also need to be able to relax, and be a little philosophical.

Although he has not confirmed this, the actor Kevin Bacon is reported to have lost $50 million in the Madoff affair. Ouch! But Bacon has displayed some real backbone in discussing the loss publicly. As he points out, he still has his health, a home, a family and a career – a lot to be grateful for. Life can go on, even after such a massive setback. Maybe we should take a leaf out of Kevin Bacon's book; ultimately, there really are many things that are more important than money.

Afterword

Some new developments in some of the stories in this book have emerged as the book was going to press, and these are discussed below. For private investors who are eager not to get cheated in the future, it pays to study how frauds were perpetrated in the past, but we should not forget that frauds are never going to disappear. There is no 'closure' in these matters; some of the guilty will go jail, and others will avoid it, but in the next financial boom it is a racing certainty that there will be new frauds, however hard the regulators try to prevent it. This is simply the way of the world; as private investors we need to remember that fraud is an ever-present possibility, and to do our best to watch out for it.

The LIBOR scandal trundles on. RBS, currently 81% owned by the British taxpayer, is said to be in negotiation with the UK and US governments over large fines, and who will pay them (various politicians have said that it should be the bankers, and not the British taxpayer). The scandal may have serious implications for the UK's financial sector and London's status as a leading global financial centre, if, as has been proposed, some of the regulation of LIBOR, or of any new reference rates that replace it, are moved to another country. So far, three major banks, Barclays, UBS, and RBS, have been implicated but more than 20 banks around the world are now the subject of investigations or court cases relating to the scandal and it seems probable that it will eventually be established that the LIBOR rate rigging was done by a cartel of major banks; in other words, that it was a systemic, institutional fraud that affected the whole world's interest rates. Reforms will come, no doubt, but with so much of the world in a shaky economic condition it may not be politically possible to achieve the radical reforms that many people would like to see.

In early June 2013 it was announced that Jefferson County was close to an agreement with its creditors to reduce and refinance its billions of dollars' worth of debt. JPMorgan Chase, in particular, is reported to have agreed to give up $842 million, some 70% of what it is owed for the sewer deals. As Robert Brooks, a professor of finance at the University of Alabama, remarked, 'I think any reasonable person would *not* come to the conclusion they're [JPMorgan Chase] just really nice people. When you inflict harm you have to make it right.' What galls many Americans is that although a number of corrupt municipal officials went to prison for their role in this mess – the largest municipal bankruptcy in American history – no one from Wall Street has been incarcerated.

The UK's FSA was abolished in April 2013. Like its US counterpart, the SEC, it failed to cover itself in glory during the 'light touch' regulatory regime of the 2000s, when many of the frauds covered in this book came to light. Not all of the criticism the FSA has received has been fair, but it is evident that it did not succeed in reining in the worst excesses of the financial sector. Sir James Crosby, CEO of HBOS until 2006, was also deputy chief of the FSA between 2006 and 2009, resigning from the latter position amid allegations by Paul Moore, head of regulatory risk at HBOS, that Crosby had fired him after Moore had warned that HBOS had been lending in a very risky way. In April 2003 the UK's parliamentary commission on banking standards said Crosby should take the primary responsibility for the near collapse of HBOS, and in June, at Crosby's request, he was formally stripped of his knighthood. HBOS's problems seem to have been more to do with wishful thinking at the top than any deliberate wrongdoing, but the fact that Crosby also held a senior position at the FSA illustrates why it became politically impossible to allow the FSA to continue as the UK's main financial regulator. The FSA will be replaced by the Financial Conduct Authority (FCA) and the Prudential Regulation Authority (PRA), who will be given new powers to prevent financial scandals. As always, the fundamental problem remains: how do you regulate the City without killing off its power to create wealth?

Now that the noughties boom is over, hedge funds are coming under increasing scrutiny. *Forbes* magazine, in a March 2013 article, suggested that, in the US, the hedge fund industry 'is overrun with unethical and illegal activity'. An anonymous survey of hedge fund managers conducted by the New York law firm Labaton Sucharow produced some interesting findings, including: 46% of respondents said that they thought that their competitors were likely to have engaged in unethical or illegal activities; 35% felt under pressure to act illegally or unethically; 30% said they had direct knowledge of wrongdoing at work; and 54% thought that the SEC was ineffective in catching and prosecuting wrongdoers. Anecdotal evidence seems to support these findings on both sides of the Atlantic. This is a section of the industry that is severely under-regulated, and it is about time that it gets cleaned up. Investors beware!

Many of the major fraudsters of the 2000s, such as Allen Stanford, are now yesterday's news, but Bernie Madoff, the biggest of them all, is still attracting attention. It seems likely that Madoff had highly-placed associates, in both the US and Europe, who have not yet been brought to justice. In June 2013 the liquidators of Madoff Securities International Limited (MSIL), which was based in London, sued a number of Madoff's relatives, Sonja Kohn, the founder of Bank Medici, and others, claiming that very large sums of money were funnelled illegally through MSIL by Madoff. A slew of books and films about the scandal – the witnesses range from a secretary to a daughter-in-law – continue to appear. Meanwhile, back in the US, Madoff himself continues to utter snippets of information suggesting that he has more to tell; for example, he has claimed that the major banks 'knew' what he was up to and has offered to testify before Congressional committees on the matter. Robert De Niro is due to star as Bernie in a major motion picture, which should be entertaining. Says De Niro, 'It's interesting how it's about trust … I think that's very interesting, that people, with all the smarts that they have about business and numbers and this … at the end of the day it's about people interacting and how he conned people.' Let's hope that De Niro can provide some deeper insights into the mind of this great villain; if any actor can, he can.

The Cyprus banking crisis, which erupted in spring 2013, has raised a spectre that many had believed was long gone: the prospect of a 'levy' (in other words, expropriation) on deposits held in Cypriot banks. This does not bode well, since it could be a precedent for more levies on deposits held in other countries, especially in troubled areas of the EU but also in other parts of the world. Such levies, which many investors regard simply as a form of theft by a government, are deeply antithetical to free market principles and are very bad news for the investment world as a whole: if you can't trust governments to run the game fairly, whom can you trust? Friends and colleagues from countries likely to be affected, such as Spain, tell me that they have already prepared for this eventuality. As the psalm says, 'Put not your trust in princes, nor in the son of man, in whom there is no help.' Investors are probably going to be in for a bumpy ride over the next few years.

Further reading

Antar, S., **www.whitecollarfraud.com** – Sam Antar's views on Crazy Eddie Inc.

Arvedlund, E., *Too Good to Be True: The Rise and Fall of Bernie Madoff*, New York, 2009.

Babiak, P. and Hare, R. D., *Snakes in Suits: When Psychopaths go to Work*, New York, 2006.

Barchard, D., *Asil Nadir and the Rise and Fall of Polly Peck*, London, 1992.

Brummer, A., *The Crunch: The Scandal of Northern Rock and the Escalating Credit Crisis*, London, 2008.

Burrough, B., 'Pirate of the Caribbean', *Vanity Fair*, Vol. 51, No.7 (3 June 2009), pp. 51-76, reprinted in Graydon Carter, *The Great Hangover: 21 Tales of the New Recession*, New York, 2010, pp. 251-275.

Butterfield, S., *Amway: the Cult of Free Enterprise*, New York, 1985.

Campbell, D., and Griffin, S., 'Enron and the End of Corporate Governance' in S. MacLeod (ed.), *Global Governance and the Quest for Justice*, Oxford, 2006, pp. 47–72.

Cleckley, H., *The Mask of Sanity*, 5th ed. St Louis, MO, 1976.

Culp, C. and Hanke, S., 'Empire of the sun: an economic interpretation of Enron's energy business', *Policy Analysis No. 470*, Cato Institute, Washington DC, 2003.

Dalmady, A., 'Duck Tales', *VenEconomy Monthly* (January 2009), pp. 11-15.

Deakin, S. and Konzelmann, S., 'After Enron: an age of enlightenment?', *Organization*, 13, 2003, pp. 583-587.

Drew, J. and Drew, M., 'Who was Swimming Naked when the Tide went out? Introducing Criminology to the Finance Curriculum', School of Criminology and Criminal Justice, Griffith University, Nathan, Australia. 2011.

Elfrink, T., 'SEC Says Texas Financier Sir Allen Stanford Swindled Investors Out of Billions', *Dallas Observer* (Texas), 9 April 2009.

Ferguson, C., Beck, C. and Bolt, A., 'Inside Job', transcript of documentary film, Sony Pictures, 2010. **www.sonyclassics.com/awards-information/insidejob_ screenplay.pdf**

FitzPatrick, R. and Reynolds, J., *False Profits: Seeking Financial and Spiritual Deliverance in Multi-Level Marketing and Pyramid Schemes*, Charlotte, N.C., 1997.

Fusaro, P. and Miller, R., *What Went Wrong at Enron*, London, 2002.

Groia, J., Badley, J. and Jones, A., *The Aftermath of Bre-X: The Industry's Reaction to the Decision and the Lessons We All Have Learned*, a paper prepared for the PDAC Conference, Toronto, March 4, 2008. **www.groiaco.com/pdf/The_Aftermath_ of_Bre-X_Mar_4-08.pdf**

Hare, R. D., *Without Conscience: The Disturbing World of Psychopaths Among Us*, New York, 1998.

Henriques, D., *The Wizard of Lies: Bernie Madoff and the Death of Trust*, London, 2011.

Herzog, A., *Vesco: From Wall Street to Castro's Cuba, the Rise, Fall, and Exile of the King of White Collar Crime*, New York, 1987.

Hodgson, G., Page, B. and Raw, C., *Do You Sincerely Want To Be Rich?*, New York, 1971.

Lawson, G., *Octopus: Sam Israel, the Secret Market, and Wall Street's Wildest Con*, New York, 2013.

Lewis, M., *Liar's Poker*, London, 1990.

Lowenstein, R., *When Genius Failed: The Rise and Fall of Long-Term Capital Management*, London, 2001.

Madoff Mack, S., *The End of Normal: A Wife's Anguish, A Widow's New Life*, New York, 2012.

Markopolos, H., *No One Would Listen: A True Financial Thriller*, Hoboken, N.J., 2010.

McLean, B. and Elkind, P., *The Smartest Guys in the Room: The Amazing Rise and Scandalous Fall of Enron*, New York, 2004.

Mollenkamp, C. and Norman, L., 'British bankers group steps up review of widely used Libor', *Wall Street Journal*, 17 April 2008, p. C7.

Mollenkamp, C. and Whitehouse, M., 'Study casts doubt on key rate; WSJ analysis suggests banks may have reported flawed interest data for Libor', *Wall Street Journal*, 29 May 2008, p. A1.

Peel, M., *Nigeria-Related Financial Crime and its links with Britain*, Chatham House, London, 2006.

SEC, 'Report of Investigation: Investigation of the SEC's Response to Concerns Regarding Robert Allen Stanford's Alleged Ponzi Scheme', United States Securities and Exchange Commission, Office of Inspector General, Case No. OIG-526, New York, 31 March 2010.

Shafir, E., Diamond, P. and Tversky, A., 'Money Illusion', *The Quarterly Journal of Economics*, Vol. 112, Issue 2, May 1997, pp 341-374.

Sorkin, A., *Too Big to Fail: The Inside Story of How Wall Street and Washington Fought to Save the Financial System--and Themselves*, New York, 2010.

Staley, K., *The Art of Short Selling*, New York, 1997.

Taibbi, M., 'Looting Main Street', *Rolling Stone*, 31 March 2010.

Valentine, D., 'Pyramid Schemes', Prepared statement presented at the International Monetary Fund's Seminar on Current Legal Issues Affecting Central Banks, Washington D.C., 13 May 1998. **www.ftc.gov/speeches/other/dvimf16.shtm**

Woodford, M., *Exposure: Inside the Olympus Scandal: How I Went from CEO to Whistleblower*, London, 2012.

Court cases

Many court documents relating to high-profile financial cases are now made available via the websites of official receivers, financial regulators, and other professional and governmental bodies, including:

www.stanfordfinancialreceivership.com
The receiver for Stanford International Bank

www.justice.gov
US Department of Justice

www.c-span.org
Excellent US public service TV, good for government hearings.

www.parliamentlive.tv/Main/Home.aspx
The UK's Parliament TV provides good coverage of recent inquiries into financial scandals.

www.madofftrustee.com
The receiver for the Madoff funds

www.fsa.gov.uk
The Financial Services Authority

www.fca.org.uk
The Financial Conduct Authority

www.bankofengland.co.uk
The Prudential Regulation Authority (PRA)

Selected cases

(Note: this is a small selection of the very large number of cases relating to the frauds covered in this book. Much of these materials are available on the internet, but as their URLs may change they are not given here – the best way to find them is by searching for the case in the websites listed above, or by using a search engine or a legal database such as LEXIS if you have access).

Pendergest-Holt *v* Certain Underwriters at Lloyd's of London, 2010 U.S. Dist. LEXIS 108920 (S.D. Tex. Oct. 13, 2010).

SEC *v* Stanford Int'l Bank, Ltd., Case No. 3:09-cv-0298-N (N.D. Tex. Mar. 12, 2009).

Adams *v* Stanford, Case No. 4:09-cv-00474 (S.D. Tex. 2009).

Stanford Group Co. *v* Tidwell (In re Stanford Group Co.), 273 S.W.3d 807 (Tex. App. Houston 14th Dist. 2008).

United States *v* Davis, Criminal Case No. H-09-335 (U.S. District Court, S.D. Tex., August 27, 2009).

United States *v* Stanford, Criminal Action No. H-09-342-1 (S.D. Tex. 2009).

Index